Violence
&
Trauma

Healing South Sudanese
Families and Communities

AKUCH KUOL ANYIETH

ISBN: 9780975630433 (Paperback)
9781763591882 (Hardcover)
9781763683921 (eBook)

Cover design, typesetting and layout: Africa World Books
Unit 3, 57 Frobisher St, Osborne Park, WA 6017
P.O. Box 1106 Osborne Park, WA 6916

ABOUT THE AUTHOR

Dr Akuch Kuol Anyieth is a crime, justice, and legal scholar. She has over a decade of experience in criminal justice, family violence practice, and trauma-informed research. Among her qualifications, Akuch holds a Bachelor of Legal Studies from La Trobe University, a Master of Justice and Criminology from RMIT University, a second Master of Arts (researching family violence), a Doctor of Philosophy (PhD) in Law and Society from La Trobe University, a qualified Trauma-Informed Coach, and completed a yearlong governance and political training at The University of Melbourne, Australia. Dr Akuch Kuol Anyieth is a Research Fellow at the Centre for the Study of the Afterlife of Violence and Reparative Quest at the University of Stellenbosch, South Africa. She is also an adjunct assistant professor at the University of Juba, South Sudan and an adjunct researcher at La Trobe University, Melbourne, Australia.

CONTENTS

I Cannot Think of All the Pains

"I cannot think of all the pains in men's breasts
without the urge to sleep, or to lie down, I cannot think
without seeing God's face in the child's smile,
or in the lonely cry in the night and in the sea.

I cannot think of all the pains that have come
and gone, pains in men's waists
and in men's shoes —
I cannot have relief proper, wearing a neat tie.

I run around in circles, like sprinkling water,
I can't have true relief, swearing out loud
and counting out the pains in my breast,
and in my pants.
I cannot think of all the pains and all the years wasted,
all the craze of lonely men in village rooms,
and all the bodies that lie out cold, in avoided streets-
I can't run out old, like a joyful child

and watch a sky pregnant with pain, or with turbulent rain;
I cannot think of the soil without lying down,
I cannot think of tears, lonely geographies
and the third world, without the urge to cry or to sit down".

- Mxolisi Nyezwa

CHAPTER 1

VIOLENCE

Unraveling the Threads of
Violence and Trauma

To truly grasp the enigma of violence and its prevention, we must adopt a psychological lens that seeks to decipher the underlying meanings behind all forms of behaviour, including the most violent. Even acts that appear irrational or insane to onlookers hold a rationale within the mind of the perpetrator. Understanding these motives becomes paramount in the pursuit of effective prevention strategies. Similarly, acts of violence that may seem rational or self-interested often emerge from deeply irrational and ultimately self-destructive impulses. The key to prevention lies in unravelling these underlying

motives and channelling them under individual and societal self-control. We must also acknowledge that the road to
understanding and resolution is not solely paved with punitive actions. Instead, we must peel back the layers of trauma,
pain, and desperation that drive violent acts. By approaching
violence as a complex and multi-faceted phenomenon, we
gain insight into the societal underpinnings that perpetuate
its existence and steps we should take towards repair, healing,
and prevention.

Several years ago, I found myself at a crossroads, grappling
with the profound impact of my experiences working closely
with countless victims, survivors, and perpetrators of violence.
It was a turning point that led me to make a decision that
was both deeply personal and professionally significant: to
share my family, my community, and our society's history
with violence. This narrative, woven with threads of pain and
resilience, would serve as a poignant backdrop for the themes
I would explore throughout this book — themes that delve
into the intricacies of violence within the South Sudanese
communities and communities with similar experiences of
war, displacement, settlement, race, and racism that lead to or
exacerbate the prevalence of violence. Its far-reaching effects
on individuals of all genders and ages, the haunting trauma
it leaves in its wake, and the ethical dilemmas that surround
its aftermath.

Within the depths of this journey, I was confronted with
a resounding truth, echoed by the eminent James Gilligan:
violence often originates at home then spread into the society

(Gilligan, 2001). The very essence of our human nature, our earliest lessons in conflict resolution, is forged within the intimate confines of our homes. It is within these crucibles that we learn the fundamental strategies for navigating life's challenges, exacerbating existing problems, and sometimes, tragically, creating entirely new ones.

As an academic embarking on a discourse on violence, I realised the profound significance of examining the roots of this complex issue from within the home – where all lives begin, where emotions and tensions intertwine, where relationships bloom or wither, and where the seeds of violence or peace are sown. This exploration seeks to uncover the intricacies of our shared human experience, recognising that the journey towards healing, repair, and understanding must begin within the very fabric of our families and communities – treating it not only as a personal issue but as a national, communal, societal, socioeconomic, social justice, and criminal justice issue.

The field of social and criminal justice often involves working with survivors of violence and other vulnerable people. These may be victims of a wide range of violent crimes, including war veterans, sexual assault, family violence, and also offenders whose situations are linked to their own histories of victimisation and abuse. This work requires insights and skills to ensure that individuals are effectively supported and protected from primary and secondary victimisation. This book offers an opportunity to discuss the perpetration of violence and victimisation within the South Sudanese communities in the diaspora while drawing on examples from the actual country, South Sudan. Through understanding the complex and destructive reactions people have to traumatic experiences, the vulnerabilities they continue to carry, and the support that might be effective in working towards repair, rehabilitation, and justice. This is provided through an integration of social, criminal justice, and political approaches to vulnerability and victimisation with critical psychological theories of trauma and key theorists on vicarious trauma. Though the book might mainly focus on South Sudan/South Sudanese, it draws on examples from other nations that have and are experiencing violence and, as a result of violence, experiencing trauma, on a reparative quest, healing, and nation-building.

In the pages that follow, we shall navigate the turbulent waters of violence, delving into the profound emotions of shame and pride entangled in its aftermath. We shall confront the haunting spectre of trauma, experienced by victims and perpetrators alike, recognising the interplay of justice and morality, crime and punishment. Throughout this narrative, the human tragedy that accompanies violence will loom large, highlighting the imperative need for healing, renewal, and transformation.

While the task ahead is heavy, it is not without hope. As we embark on this journey, we shall also encounter stories of resilience, courage, and the indomitable human spirit. It is through these stories that we shall find glimmers of light amidst the darkness, reminding us that transformation is indeed possible, even in the face of the most profound adversity.

As we peer into the depths of violence and trauma, let us

keep in mind the shared responsibility we hold as a society. The lessons we uncover here go far beyond the realm of academia - they call upon us to collectively shape a world where safety and healing are prioritised, where resources are allocated to support the wellbeing of all, where criminal justice approaches are not the only solutions to crime prevention, and where the cycle of transferred trauma is broken. It is a challenge that requires us to introspect, to examine our own roles, and to carry the willingness to repair and to heal, individually, as a community, and as a global society.

With each chapter, I will weave a tapestry of understanding, root causes of violence, and action towards repair, seeking to mend the frayed edges of our collective humanity. In this pursuit, may we emerge not only with a profound understanding of violence and its effects but also with a vision for a future where violence is replaced by peace and empathy, where trauma finds solace in healing and repair, and where the seeds of peaceful coexistence are sown.

As my understanding of diverse lives expanded, a stark truth began to emerge - hardly any family history was untouched by the haunting spectre of fatal or life-threatening violence. Whether in the form of suicide, homicide, femicide, death in combat, or other non-natural occurrences, human violence manifested itself in a myriad of tragic ways, leaving deep scars upon the fabric of society. It became evident that violence, in its complexity and tragedy, surpassed the common recognition it receives.

Despite the wealth of literature on violence from esteemed

experts in criminology, criminal law, forensic psychiatry, moral philosophy, political science, and history, a critical understanding of its deeply rooted origins often eluded us. While those directly immersed in the daily struggles against individual violence - judges, lawyers, criminologists, forensic psychiatrists, law enforcement officers, and prison administrators - bore witness to its profound impact, professional discussions rarely allowed space for the articulation of a personal viewpoint. The focus predominantly centred on moral and legal aspects through the lens of the criminal justice system, limiting our comprehension of violence and hindering other forms of effective prevention.

Bearing witness to the current unfolding wars and many harsh disasters in the world, we can all agree that violent histories, whether physical, structural, or transgenerational trauma, are destructive to human existence and coexistence. I aim to bring conceptual as well as practical clarity to the concept of violence and its consequences in the lives of victim and survivor groups on the one hand, and perpetrators and their descendants on the other. I take an intersectional approach and engage with the physical and structural aspects of violence, as well as the more insidious and symbolic forms of its expression that manifest in dynamic ways. I aim to put the issue of repair in the aftermath of violent histories at the centre and to explore and examine various strategies that can be employed to heal the past.

Within the shadows of this harsh reality lies a glimmer of hope and a path towards healing and prevention. Conventional approaches often lean towards punitive measures, such as increasing police presence, imposing harsher sentences, and building more prisons. Yet, a more profound and meaningful approach calls for healing individuals and investing in preventive measures that address the roots of violence.

At the core of this exploration lies a call for repair - healing for victims and perpetrators alike, healing for families fractured by violence, and healing for communities besieged by its enduring consequences. In embracing this path of healing, we open the door to a future where violence is no longer an inevitable thread woven into the fabric of society. By shifting our focus towards repair and prevention, we envision a world where the roots of violence are identified and addressed early on. This involves investing in resources that bolster emotional resilience, support mental well-being, and nurture healthy relationships. It calls for a collective effort to break the cycles of violence and to nurture a culture of empathy, understanding, and compassion.

In the chapters that follow, we shall embark on a journey of exploration and introspection, guided by the light of knowledge and fuelled by the urgency for change. My mission is not merely to comprehend the complexities of violence but to pave the way for a future where healing and prevention stand at the forefront of our efforts. As I navigate through the labyrinth of human violence, let us be guided by the voices of both victims and perpetrators, acknowledging their pain and their shared humanity. Together, we shall weave a tapestry of transformation, embracing healing, compassion, and the pursuit of a violence-free world.

In the unique context of South Sudanese communities, violence takes on a distressing and deeply entrenched form. Merely viewing violent crime in isolation fails to address the broader patterns of violence that have become accepted and normalized within society. To truly comprehend the issue, we must shift our focus from mere criminality to a comprehensive analysis of the societal and psychological roots of violence. By delving into the heart of South Sudanese communities, we uncover the intricate interplay of historical traumas, social norms, and individual struggles that contribute to the perpetuation of violence. The result is a group of profoundly hurt people living with multiple layers of traumatic distress, chronic anxiety, physical ill-health, mental distress, fears, depressions, substance abuse, and now the high imprisonment rates of our young people. Through this lens, it becomes evident that violence is not solely a matter of individual actions; it is a reflection of a complex web of influences that shape behaviours and perceptions.

In this pursuit, I come to realise the urgent need for alternative approaches that go beyond traditional law enforcement and punitive measures. Prevention demands a multi-faceted strategy that addresses the underlying issues driving violence. It calls for empathy, compassion, and a profound understanding of the human psyche. By examining violence from a social and psychological perspective, we are equipped to untangle the threads of trauma and despair that bind individuals to violent acts. Understanding the intricate web of emotions, beliefs, and experiences that fuel violence empowers us to craft interventions tailored to healing and repair.

Prevention, thus, becomes an endeavour that extends beyond reactive responses. It involves engaging communities in dialogue, fostering resilience, and providing avenues for healing. It means confronting the wounds of the past and working collectively to build a future anchored in peace and understanding. As I illuminate the darkness surrounding violence, I recognize that prevention requires a holistic approach that addresses not just the symptoms but the roots. It necessitates an exploration of the societal norms and structures that have unwittingly perpetuated violence for generations. By embracing this profound social and psychological perspective, we embark on a path of transformation, where violence is no longer seen as an inevitable outcome, but as a problem with possible actionable solutions that can prevent and ultimately be eradicated. Together, we shall build a future that cherishes the sanctity of human life and celebrates the power of collective initiatives to repair society."

Before we embark on this profound exploration of violence within South Sudan and its diaspora, it is imperative to confront and dispel the deeply ingrained stereotype of Africa's association with violence – a notion often referred to as Afro-nihilism. This stereotype, born from a history marred by colonisation, enslavement, and oppression, unfairly taints the collective image of the entire continent. It fails to acknowledge the distinct historical contexts and unique experiences of countries like Sudan and South Sudan, two of the world's youngest nations.

Understanding the traumas and vulnerabilities that these

nations have endured throughout their histories is crucial in comprehending their present actions and challenges. Their struggles for independence, sovereignty, and self-determination have shaped their collective identity and their journey towards healing and growth. As we venture into the heart of South Sudanese communities, my aim is not to perpetuate the stereotype, but to unravel the intricate web of violence and trauma that grips the nation and the South Sudanese people here in the diaspora. It is a journey of profound empathy and understanding, seeking to shed light on the significance of recognising violence as a tragedy.

By adopting a broader perspective that transcends geographical boundaries, I recognize that violence is not confined to a particular region or ethnicity; it is a universal human affliction that knows no borders. Embracing this truth enables us to forge a path towards healing, not only for South Sudan but for all communities impacted by violence around the world. Within the depths of violence lie the untold stories of suffering, loss, and pain – stories that demand to be heard with sensitivity and compassion. It is in listening to these narratives, in acknowledging the wounds of the past, that we can begin to envision a future free from the chains of violence.

Breaking the cycle of violence requires collective effort and a commitment to empathy and understanding. By challenging the Afro-nihilism stereotype, I reject the notion that violence is an inherent trait of African communities. Instead, I acknowledge the resilience and strength that lie within each individual, capable of transcending the traumas of history and forging a new path of healing. Through this exploration, I strive to dismantle the walls of division and build bridges of understanding, compassion, and empathy. Together, we can create a world where violence is recognized as a tragedy and healing is embraced as the path towards a brighter and more peaceful future. Let us embark on this journey with open hearts and open minds, for only then can we truly make a difference in the lives of those impacted by violence, in war-torn countries, in communities, and families experiencing the perpetration of violence.

Violence is Not Instinctual: The Fallacy of Innate Violence

In the vast tapestry of human history, a longstanding theory has woven itself into the fabric of our understanding—violence as an instinctual part of our nature. This notion proposes that within each of us lurks an untamed beast, a residue of our animal ancestry, predisposing us to act aggressively and violently (Clare, 1969; Fields, 2019). But is this theory really as captivating as it seems, or is it a myth waiting to be unravelled?

Imagine, for a moment, a world where violent impulses build up within us like a tempest, seeking release through predetermined, inherited patterns of behaviour. This idea, championed by influential thinkers like Freud (1915), offers an explanation that may seem seductive at first glance. Even students of animal behaviour, including the likes of Lorenz (1966) and E.O. Wilson (1980), have echoed this tune, attributing violence to deeply ingrained, instinctual drives.

Yet, as we delve deeper into the heart of this mystery, we encounter cracks in such theory—flaws that unravel its enchanting facade. The venerable ethologist, N. Tinbergen (1942; 1951), raises a compelling and thought-provoking question about the enduring significance of the term "instinct." In our pursuit of understanding the intricate mechanisms governing behaviour, he questions whether we may have clung too tightly to this concept, rendering it somewhat vague and indiscriminate in its application. Instead, Tinbergen advocates for a shift towards a more precise and illuminating notion— that of "fixed-action patterns."

Intriguingly, Tinbergen juxtaposes the stark differences between the behaviours of animals and humans. While animals often exhibit innate, unlearned behaviours dictated by specific environmental triggers, human conduct boasts unparalleled flexibility and adaptability. This dynamic characteristic sets us apart from our animal counterparts, making the idea of "instinct" seem somewhat inadequate when attempting to comprehend the intricacies of human behaviour.

With great insight, Tinbergen postulates that terms like "instinct" encompass broad classes of behaviours, blurring the distinct actions that each behaviour entails. For instance, the classification of activities such as fighting, gregariousness, and self-assertion as single, definite behaviour patterns may fall short in capturing the rich tapestry of nuanced actions that form the basis of human conduct. Instead, he proposes that we embrace the notion of "fixed-action patterns," which better capture the innate, pre-programmed behaviours observed in various animal species. Such a shift in perspective reminds us of the intricate interplay between innate tendencies and the capacity for adaptability inherent in human behaviour. Tinbergen's advocacy for a more precise language of description in the study of behaviour challenges us to delve deeper into the complexities of our actions, veering away from overly generalised concepts that may obscure crucial distinctions.

As we ponder the implications of Tinbergen's perspective, we are encouraged to reevaluate our understanding of human behaviour and its underlying drivers. By embracing the concept of "fixed-action patterns," we unlock the potential for a more refined and profound comprehension of the intricacies that define human conduct, leaving us with a richer and more illuminating narrative of our species' behavioural tendencies.

What if, contrary to the symphony of instincts, violence doesn't follow a uniform rhythm? Experts like L. Bernard Luther (1922) reveal that terms like fighting, gregariousness, and self-assertion encompass a multitude of concrete mechanisms, none of which truly coalesce into a single unitary behaviour pattern. Thus, the notion of a violent instinct becomes entangled in the complexities of our psyche, presenting more questions than answers.

Leading investigators of animal aggression, such as J. P. Scott, boldly challenge the idea of an aggressive instinct akin to hunger, for there are no discernible patterns or measurable internal triggers for such violent impulses. It seems that the allure of an instinctual explanation for violence may be fading, leaving behind a void to be filled by a deeper understanding.

Venturing further into this complex puzzle, we discover that this theory can lead us astray, shrouding our path with pessimism. The belief that violence is hardwired into our being may diminish hope for change, as it suggests we are bound by fate. However, peering through the haze, we find that violence is a product of complex social dynamics and individual choices, rendering it amenable to alteration. Ah, but beware the sirens of release! The theory also provokes with the promise that violent impulses can be discharged through non-lethal outlets. The allure of aggressive sports, economic rivalries, and competitive ventures may seem like a safe harbour, but it is a dangerous illusion. These mere outlets fail to address the underlying cultural values that perpetuate violence, concealing the real beast lurking beneath.

Intriguingly, the widespread acceptance of this theory may be more entangled in human psychology than meets the eye. Justifying political conservatism and the status quo, it veils the possibility of transformative change. As we peel away the layers of this captivating narrative, we find the need to move beyond recycling violence and embrace a new dawn of true resolution.

In this exhilarating journey of revelation, we must recognize the essence of our shared humanity. Cast aside notions of aggression and savagery, and embrace a culture of repair. For beneath the surface, regardless of gender, race, or social class, lies the core of vulnerability—a universal yearning for care and support.

As we unravel the myth of innate violence, the landscape of our understanding transforms. Instead of submitting to the appeal of the beast within, let us aspire to transcend it and nurture a world where violence fades into the annals of history, while we repair and build a safer society.

CHAPTER 2

A ROAD FROM HELL

As we embark on our expedition into the heart of South Sudan's turbulent history, let me emphasise that I do not perceive this nation as hell itself. Rather, it symbolises the starting point of our profound exploration into the legacies of violence that have shaped our destinies. In this chapter, aptly titled "Road from Hell," I embark on a compelling journey to unearth the roots and delve into the mythological dimensions of the pressing issue that has left indelible marks on the lives and minds of victims, survivors, and perpetrators of violence.

In this quest for understanding, we must tread carefully through the annals of time, tracing the intricate threads of violence that have woven themselves into the fabric of South Sudanese society and its people. The road we traverse is not merely one of geographical landscapes, but of emotional, social, and psychological landscapes as well – a terrain fraught with complexities, contradictions, and untold narratives.

As we venture forth, we must be prepared to encounter harrowing accounts of suffering and resilience, stories of triumph over adversity, and the haunting echoes of past traumas that linger in the present. The road from hell was not a straightforward path; it is a labyrinth of intertwined destinies, where the past and present converge to shape the future.

In our expedition, we shall encounter the ghosts of history, those shadows of the past that continue to cast their long reach over the present. We shall confront the legacies of colonization, the scars of war and conflict, and the struggles for independence and identity. Each bend in the road holds a story waiting to be told, a story that offers glimpses into the human condition and the indomitable spirit that defies the darkness. But let us not be deterred by the enormity of the task ahead, for within the heart of darkness lies the potential for transformation and healing. As we venture deeper into the core of South Sudan's collective psyche, we shall also unearth tales of hope, resilience, and the power of human connection.

This journey is not one for the faint of heart, as it demands courage to confront the uncomfortable truths that lie beneath the surface. Yet, it is a journey worth embarking upon, for within the depths of this exploration lies the opportunity to shed light on the shadows, acts of violence, dysfunctions, and pave the way for a brighter future.

The Road from Hell was not a solitary path; it is a road we travel together, hand in hand, fostering understanding and empathy for one another's experiences. It is a road that calls for compassion and a willingness to listen, for it is through the power of genuine connection that healing and reconciliation can begin. As we embark on this chapter, let us do so with open minds and open hearts, ready to bear witness to the stories of South Sudan's past and present. It is only by acknowledging the road that has led us here that we can chart a new course towards a future where violence is not destiny, and where the scars of history can finally find solace in the embrace of healing.

To delve into the realm of violence and its destructive traumas is to confront a veritable inferno, reminiscent of the chilling tales of Golgotha, the horrors of Auschwitz and Armenia, the dark chapters of Andersonville and Attica, the harrowing "Middle Passage," and the tragic massacre at Wounded Knee, also known as the Battle of Wounded Knee (1890), and events like the 1993 Sudan famine (Hynd & de Waal, 1997) and the Rwandan genocide (1994) (Hintjens, 1999). These are the stories that sear our souls as humans and challenge us to ask ourselves whether we possess the courage to face such a terrible reality and embark on this journey together.

The chilling tales of Golgotha mirror the images where communities have faced immense suffering and sacrifice. Like the anguish of King Lear, Sudan and South Sudan have experienced the tragic consequences of unchecked power, betrayal, and conflict, leading to immense pain and devastation for its people. The horrors of the civil war find echoes in the memories of Sudanese communities who have endured grave human rights violations and vile acts, leaving deep scars on the collective memory of the nation and its people across the globe.

Similarly, the dark chapters of Andersonville and Attica resonate with Sudan's history of political unrest, civil wars, and the mistreatment of prisoners and civilians during various conflicts. The harrowing "Middle Passage" evokes the displacement and suffering of Sudanese people during forced migrations and refugee crises. Lastly, the tragic massacre at Wounded Knee draws parallels to incidents of violence and bloodshed that have plagued Sudan's past. These haunting tales sear the souls of those who have witnessed or experienced such traumas, prompting us to confront the reality of violence and its far-reaching impacts on Sudan and South Sudanese society. As we embark on this collective journey, we must summon the courage to confront these painful truths and work towards healing, reconciliation, and a future free from the chains of violence.

In our exploration of violence, we are faced with the intricate tapestry of human history, woven with threads of conflict, conquest, and suffering. The histories of Sudan/South Sudan's past bear witness to the rise and fall of empires, territorial disputes, and power struggles that have left indelible scars on the collective memory. We must tread carefully, for beneath the surface of this turbulent history lies a deeper understanding of the forces that have shaped the nation's identity and culture.

In this chapter, I embark on a daring expedition, guided by the ancient whispers of myths and legends that have threaded their way through the tapestry of South Sudanese culture.

My quest is to illuminate the mythological dimensions of violence and unearth the narratives that have perpetuated its cycle through generations. As we venture forth, we find ourselves traversing a landscape where reality and mythology intertwine, creating a potent brew of beliefs and traditions that have shaped the course of history. These stories, passed down through time like sacred heirlooms, offer profound insights into the origins and perpetuation of violence within the heart of South Sudan.

In the shadows of these ancient tales, we encounter the ghosts of those who have borne witness to the horrors of war and conflict. Their ethereal presence serves as a poignant reminder of the traumas etched into the collective memory of the nation. Their voices echo through the annals of time, beckoning us to explore the very essence of violence's genesis. For centuries, these myths have seeped into the consciousness of South Sudanese society, influencing perceptions of power, honour, and retribution. The legends of brave warriors and epic battles have woven a narrative that glorifies aggression and valorises the use of force. These stories, steeped in bloodshed, have become a bedrock of cultural identity, intertwining notions of bravery and honour with the violent echoes of the past. However, while we owe not to forget our national "heroes" in other words, freedom fighters on one hand, we must also ask ourselves individually and as a society on the other hand, how we can collectively and individually break free from the shackles of this violence-breeding trauma.

Yet, as I delve deeper into the mythological realms, I uncover more than tales of conquest and heroism. I find stories of loss, suffering, and the human cost of war. Among the echoes of battle cries, we hear the anguished laments of families torn apart by conflict and the haunting cries of innocent lives lost. Our expedition compels us to question the role of these myths in perpetuating the cycle of violence. How have these stories shaped the collective psyche, influencing notions of justice, revenge, and masculinity? Are these myths merely reflections of historical events, or do they possess a deeper, symbolic resonance that continues to shape behaviour and attitudes in the present?

As we grapple with these questions, we must remain vigilant against the appeal of romanticising violence in the name of tradition. This journey calls for critical introspection and a willingness to confront uncomfortable truths. It demands that we challenge the narratives that may inadvertently perpetuate cycles of harm and pain. As we gain a deeper understanding of the mythological dimensions of violence, we begin to untangle the threads that bind us to its tragic legacy. We will realise that narratives can evolve, that new stories of resilience and reconciliation can emerge to guide us toward a future free from the shackles of violence. Together, we venture forth, holding the torch of truth, as I strive to shed light on the myths that have shaped our history. Our mission is to break free from the allure of violence and forge a new path—a path paved with compassion, empathy, and a commitment to healing the wounds of the past while preparing for the future.

In the chapters that lie ahead, I shall confront the myths and realities that have defined South Sudan's narrative. I will challenge the ghosts of violence that haunt our collective consciousness and seek a future where the echoes of war are repaired and perhaps replaced with peace. Let us embark on this transformative journey with open hearts, knowing that only by understanding our past can we chart a course toward a brighter, more violence-free future.

Through the lens of trauma research, community observations, and personal encounters, I gain insight into the motivations that drive both perpetrators and victims of violence. The wounds of shame and humiliation suffered in the past become the catalysts for revenge and a twisted pursuit of justice. Anger, fuelled by one's sense of injustice, transpires into violence – in this sense, an act of violence becomes a cry for justice. We witness how the echoes of historical trauma reverberate through generations, leaving scars that manifest in destructive behaviours and intergenerational cycles of violence.

As I navigate this road to healing and repair, I encounter South Sudanese refugees seeking solace in foreign lands. Their journey is fraught with barriers and challenges, and while they find safety from physical harm, the invisible wounds of trauma remain unaddressed. Mental health and emotional well-being often take a back seat to immediate physical needs, leaving the deeper scars unattended. The weight of collective trauma extends far beyond individual experiences, seeping into the very roots of families and communities. Its insidious influence pervades the fabric of society, leaving no aspect untouched. The repercussions of unaddressed trauma are profound, shaping attitudes, behaviour, and relationships on a collective level.

Within families, the scars of trauma can become intergenerational burdens, passed down from one generation to the next like a haunting legacy. Children who grow up in households marred by violence or conflict are often deeply affected by the emotional wounds of their parents or ancestors (Rieder & Elbert, 2013). Unresolved traumas create an atmosphere of fear, mistrust, and instability, affecting how individuals form attachments and navigate the world around them.

Communities, too, bear the burden of collective trauma. The echoes of historical atrocities reverberate through generations, creating a cycle of violence that becomes ingrained in the social fabric. Divisions may arise between different groups within the community, perpetuating animosity and preventing true reconciliation. The impact of collective trauma on attitudes and behaviours cannot be overstated. It can breed a culture of violence, where aggression and hostility are normalised as coping mechanisms. People may become desensitised to the suffering of others, perpetuating a cycle of harm and revenge that perpetuates itself through time. In trauma, the self feels fragmented, resulting in a sense of loss of identity (Rieder & Elbert, 2013). The fragmented self is unable to establish and maintain stable relationships.

In relationships, the aftermath of collective trauma can strain connections between individuals. Communication may break down, and empathy may wane as people struggle to cope with their own pain and distress. Trust, a foundation of healthy relationships, may become fragile or non-existent, hindering the ability to form meaningful connections. Furthermore, the progress and development of the human family are stunted by unhealed collective trauma. Emotional scars act as barriers to personal growth and hinder the potential for positive change. Individuals and societies grappling with the weight of their traumatic history may find it challenging to move forward, remaining trapped in patterns of conflict and strife (Murthy & Lakshminarayana, 2006). The toll on the natural world is equally significant. A society grappling with unresolved trauma may find it challenging to prioritise environmental conservation and sustainable practices. The focus on immediate survival and the perpetuation of violence may overshadow the need to protect the environment for future generations. This kind of suffering creates a multifaceted impact on individuals and communities' existence, where lives are threatened from multiple angles.

Addressing collective trauma is not only essential for healing individuals but also for building a thriving and harmonious society. Recognising and acknowledging the impact of trauma on families and communities is the first step towards breaking the cycle of violence. Providing support and resources for healing can lead to the transformation of attitudes and behaviours, fostering a more compassionate and empathetic community. Healing collective trauma requires a collective effort. It calls for courageous conversations, empathy, and a commitment to seeking reconciliation and repair. By acknowledging the pain of the past, communities can begin to build bridges of understanding and work towards a future free from the burdens of violence.

The impact of collective trauma on families and communities is immense and far-reaching. It shapes the very essence of society, influencing attitudes, behaviour, and relationships. Unresolved trauma hinders personal and societal growth, perpetuating cycles of violence and division. However, with dedication to healing and reconciliation, societies can emerge stronger and more united, ready to embrace a future that is compassionate, peaceful, and sustainable for generations to come.

In the depths of despair and darkness, hope emerges as a radiant beacon, guiding us towards a path of healing and transformation. As we confront the legacy of violence and trauma, we unveil the potential for redemption and renewal. It is through this profound exploration of our past that we can pave the way towards a brighter future.

One of the key aspects to address is the prevailing notion of heroism being associated with destruction and violence. Throughout history, society has glorified those who excel in warfare and conflict, perpetuating a dangerous myth that violence is a noble pursuit. We must challenge this perspective and redefine what it means to be a hero. True heroism lies not in inflicting harm upon others, but in seeking peaceful resolutions and showing compassion and empathy towards fellow human beings.

In the face of conflicts and disputes, we must explore alternative paths to resolution. Violence may offer a momentary release for pent-up emotions, but it only begets more pain and suffering in the long run. It is time to embrace non-violent means of resolving conflicts, engaging in dialogue, and finding common ground. By acknowledging the humanity in one another, we can break down the barriers that divide us and move towards understanding and reconciliation.

Breaking free from the chains of violence requires a collective effort. It calls for a shared commitment to repair from all sectors and its key decision-makers, and a willingness to let go of past grievances. It may be a difficult and demanding journey, but the destination is worth the effort—a society free from the shackles of violence, where individuals can thrive in harmony. To forge a new path towards peace and reconciliation, we must foster empathy and compassion within ourselves and our communities. By cultivating understanding and a sense of interconnectedness, we can build bridges of trust and cooperation. It is through these bonds that we can dismantle the walls that separate us and build a foundation of peace.

In conclusion, amidst the darkness and devastation caused by violence and trauma, hope shines as a guiding light. By challenging the notion of heroism tied to destruction and seeking alternative paths to resolving conflicts, we can break free from the chains of violence and embark on a transformative journey towards repair, healing, justice, and peace. This is a collective endeavour that demands empathy, understanding, and a commitment to building a world where violence has no place.

I urge us not to avert our gaze from the horrors that have transpired, but to confront them with courage and compassion. The road from hell may be treacherous, but it is a journey worth undertaking if we are to fully repair the current and build a peaceful future. As we traverse this path together, let us emerge stronger, wiser, and more united, paving the way for a future free from the burdens of violence and the shadows of the past. Our responses to violence are as diverse and complex as the subject itself. We may recoil in horror and revulsion, feeling outraged by the very notion of violence. Yet, paradoxically, we may also find ourselves inexplicably drawn to its darker allure, captivated by the disturbing fascination it evokes. It is a subject that both repels and captivates, forcing us to confront our own inner complexities and biases.

As we contemplate the nature of violence and its multifaceted effects, we must resist the temptation to distance ourselves from it, dismissing it as a problem solely belonging to others. In reality, violence affects us all, directly or indirectly, and each of us carries within a personal theory of violence that shapes our attitudes, behaviours, and judgments. Some may argue that violence is an aberration, an attribute only exhibited by a select few who are mentally disturbed or culturally deviant. Yet, history has often glorified the heroism of violent acts, commemorating those who excel in the art of destruction as revered war heroes. However, in light of our current knowledge, we must question the viability of violence as a survival strategy for humanity in our modern societies.

The effects of violence are far-reaching, stretching beyond individual traumas to impact entire communities, generations, and the fabric of society itself. Refugees arriving in new lands bear the weight of their psychological damage, scarred by their traumatic pasts, yet facing the challenges of settling into unfamiliar territories. Unfortunately, the support systems they encounter often overlook the invisible wounds of trauma, focusing primarily on physical well-being while neglecting mental health.

Through my professional, community, and research experiences, I personally encountered individuals touched by violence, witnessing firsthand the profound pain etched into the lives of victims, survivors, and even perpetrators. It compelled me to reevaluate my own commitment to confront this subject with unwavering clarity and sensitivity.

Survival in the face of trauma may lead individuals to suppress and avoid addressing their past experiences. For many refugees fleeing war, the quest for safety and refuge becomes a priority, often at the expense of healing. However, trauma, whether hidden in the subconscious or consciously suppressed, has a way of resurfacing, manifesting in various aspects of life, both individual and collective.

My endeavour in this book is to shed light on the historical, structural, and individual violence rooted in traumas and mental health issues among the South Sudanese people. An understanding which can be applied to many other similar communities with war, refugee, and migration experiences in the diaspora. I aim to connect the missing links between unhealed collective and individual traumas and the afflictions that extend to personal lives, culture, and society at large. The unaddressed wounds of the past continue to echo in the present, impacting the health of individuals, communities, social justice systems, and the environment.

Let us embark on this journey together as we explore the path that led to the current state of affairs in South Sudan and seek to understand the impact of violence and trauma on its people in South Sudanese and those abroad in Western countries such as Australia. It is my hope that through these lenses, we can form a deeper understanding which can then be translated into appropriate and sustainable forms of interventions and prevention of violence.

CHAPTER 3

COLONIAL INSPIRED CIVIL WARS

In order to understand the depth of these echoes of violence and trauma among the Sudanese/South Sudanese, it is important to lay out a brief historical account of colonial history that inspired division and violence, which enrobes Sudan and South Sudan today. As we embark on this tumultuous chapter, we find ourselves standing at the crossroads of time, where the echoes of colonial violence reverberate through the ages. Like ancient ruins, these haunting remnants of the past lay the groundwork for understanding the deep-rooted experiences of violence and traumas that still plague the South Sudanese community today. Within this landscape of historical turmoil, we encounter a violent state, where fractures and divisions have long been the norm.

In the annals of Sudanese history, we encounter a colossal landmass, a vast canvas painted with the intricate tapestry of power struggles and religious inspirations. It was a place where the ruling elite, fuelled by racial and religious biases, held sway, promoting their narrow interests while others bore the brunt of oppression. As Sudan gained independence from British rule in 1956, the North monopolized power, leaving the South marginalized and disenfranchised. Questions loom like spectres in the night, as we wonder how this once unified land fell into the abyss of irreparable conflict.

To unearth the origins of this strife, we must trace the tangled threads of political and religious division that date back to the days of Arab slave merchants and the oppressive rule of the Anglo-Egyptians. A colonial era of ethno-political hatred took root, sowing the seeds of discord between the North and South. The Turko-Egyptian regime, which reigned from 1821 to 1898, left indelible scars on the land (Deng, 2020). They favoured the Muslims of the North, deeming the Southerners as infidels and primitive people, intensifying the chasm between the regions.

Within this cauldron of injustice, the African in Southern Sudan lived a peripheral existence, grappling with oppression that spanned centuries (Khalid, 1990). The colonisers' insatiable greed for slaves led to pillage, the decimation of tribal communities, and extortion of taxes (Johnson, 2003a). The enslaved populations were denigrated and dehumanized, justifying their cruel fate. As the dark clouds of slavery spread, the distance between North and South grew, and unity became an illusion.

The subsequent British rule between 1898 and 1956 further fuelled disparities (Johnson, 2003a). The North prospered under the colonizers' favour, while the South remained neglected. The impact of these oppressive systems was nothing short of an atrocious drama, with bitterness and resistance taking root and poisoning the relations between North and South.

In this labyrinth of historical complexities, it becomes clear that violence and traumas in South Sudan have colonial ancient roots. The wounds of the past continue to shape the present, and the echoes of history still resonate in the hearts of the South Sudanese people. As we delve into the pages of time, we must ask ourselves: Can we break free from the chains of this colonial legacy? Can we forge a new path towards repairing the damage, reconciliation, and peace, where the scars of the past serve as lessons rather than burdens? The journey ahead is arduous, but it is one we must undertake together, holding on to hope like a flickering flame in the midst of darkness.

As the 18th century neared its end, the sinister legacy of the Turko-Egyptian colonizers loomed large, and the flames of slave raiding engulfed Southern tribes (Wai, 1981 & Deng, 2020). In this dark chapter of history, the ethnic and religious affinity between the Turko-Egyptian rulers and Arab nomads served as a malevolent force, driving the dehumanizing practice of slave-hunting (Khalid, 1990; 2003 & Deng, 2020). The haunting echoes of anguish and suffering reverberate through time, reminding us that the ramifications of this normative framework continue to plague Sudan, leaving the non-Muslim and non-Arab groups as the most marginalised and oppressed in present times.

The geographical proximity between the Egyptian rulers and the North further exacerbated the divisions between the Turko-Egyptian and the rest of Sudan (Khalid, 1990). The cordial relations shared between these rulers and the Northern tribes magnified their animosity toward Southerners, who stood apart with their distinct religious and ethnic identities (Khalid, 1990). The rise of powerful sheiks among the Northern elite, responsible for organizing slave raids and collecting taxes, marked the emergence of a class of religious rulers, consolidating power and wealth at the expense of the vulnerable.

The cruel grasp of oppression tightened, as the best farming lands were wrenched from local communities and bestowed upon district governors and sheiks, condemning Southerners to a life of enslavement or servitude (Deng, 2020). The echoes of tragedy reverberated in 1881 when the religion-political Mahdist group unleashed a popular revolt, toppling the Turko-Egyptian rule and ushering in the British colonial era (Johnson, 2003a).

As the British took the reins, a shift in rulers occurred, but the echoes of prejudice and inequality remained. The colonialists perceived Southerners as inferior and geopolitically insignificant, preferring to educate the Arabs while turning a blind eye to the Africans (Johnson, 2003a). The British administration ostensibly aimed to unify Sudan politically, but in reality, they governed the North and South separately, implementing what came to be known as the 'Southern Policy' (Deng, 2020). This policy offered some respite to the Southerners from Arab contempt and slavery while hinting at the possibility of a separate 'Negroid nation' or annexation to East Africa (Holt, 1956).

The 'Southern Policy' sought to create self-contained racial and tribal units based on indigenous customs and beliefs, thereby reinforcing Arab-Muslim domination while introducing Christian missionary education and rudiments of Western civilization in the South (Deng, 2020). The North was portrayed as 'oriental,' the epitome of civilization, while the South was demeaned as a 'people without history,' branded black, heathen, and primitive.

Racism and bigotry found fertile ground in the minds of the colonizers, who perpetuated demeaning stereotypes, relegating the Southern Sudanese to the status of child-like beings (Khalid, 1990). The pernicious curse of slavery legitimized the subjugation of black Africans, fostering a tragic history marred by cruelty and suffering.

Despite the British administration's claim of unity, their policies were tainted by racism and a sense of dominion from the very beginning of colonization (Amir Idris, 2001, p. 16). The words of Lord Cramer, the British Consul-General of Egypt, reveal the extent of this bias, with his disparaging view of Southerners as untamed primitives.

The policy of favouritism and the administration's preference for the North led to various problems, including the exclusion of Arabs and the active elimination of their influence in the South (Deng, 2020). Southern Sudan, physically distant from the Northern region, faced the challenges of inadequate transport infrastructure that hindered economic exploitation, contrasting sharply with the advantages enjoyed by the North.

The British rulers, in an effort to consolidate control, established the elite core of English administrators known as 'the Sudan Political Service' (SPS) (Johnson, 2003a). These English administrators were trained in Arabic, enabling them to serve as district authorities. However, even with the effectiveness of the SPS, Lord Cramer sought reliable Sudanese intermediaries to facilitate his dominion, often favouring highly educated Northerners for these roles.

The chapter of South Sudan's colonial history unfolds like a tapestry woven with threads of oppression, racism, and power dynamics. The struggles of the marginalised continue to resonate, reminding us that the scars of the past still shape the present. As we delve deeper into the annals of history, we must seek understanding and empathy, for only then can we hope to pave a path towards healing and reconciliation.

The vision of an educated and unified Sudan found its embodiment in the majestic Gordon Memorial College, standing tall as a symbol of enlightenment in 1902. Within its walls, Northerners were groomed and nurtured with high-quality education akin to that of Europe, crafting a generation of leaders like Ismail al-Azhari, the nation's first Prime Minister (Atiyah, 1946). Yet, the shadows of discrimination and prejudice darkened the prospects for the South, leaving them bereft of formal institutions and modern infrastructure.

The forced construction of Sudanese nationalism, akin to a puppeteer's strings, manipulated the people into believing in a unified identity that was anything but genuine. The scars of the legacy of slavery etched deep within the nation, forging an identity that labelled the North as slave masters and the South as mere hunting grounds for slaves.

The British departure in 1956 only served to unveil the profound unfairness that had been woven into the fabric of the nation. A mere six out of eight hundred vacant governmental positions were offered to the Southern population, constituting a quarter of the Sudanese populace, perpetuating the vicious cycle of exclusion (Deng, 1978). The seeds of a protracted armed conflict were sown, taking the form of the Anyanya rebellion (1955-72), a cry for justice and a demand for a share of power.

Rebellion, like a sharpened blade, became the weapon of choice for the people of South Sudan, a canvas on which the dramatic saga of war and agency unfolded. Each stroke of defiance etched the tales of struggle and resistance, painting a vivid picture of the intricate post-colonial histories that shaped the destiny of the land. The rebellion was no simple act of defiance; it was a symphony of local circumstances orchestrating the movement. The unique backdrop of South Sudan's history, forged by the colonial legacy, colonial rulers, and the deep-seated scars of oppression, played an instrumental role in the composition of this rebellion.

At the heart of this profound historical narrative lies the analysis of the colonial rulers' legacy, a key that unlocks the door to understanding the complex layers of rebellion and the institutional void in South Sudan. Like a lens of clarity, it provides the perspective through which the multifaceted history of the land can be truly comprehended.

This lens transcends the boundaries of mere national ideologies, delving deeper into the intricate tapestry of interconnected forces that shaped the course of events. It reveals how the ghosts of the past continue to haunt the present, influencing the path of the nation even beyond the realms of its borders. Through this lens, we see the imprint of colonial exploitation, the scars of discrimination, and the longing for self-determination. We witness the resilience of a people who refused to be shackled by the chains of oppression. The rebellion, a powerful and poignant expression of their agency, stands as a testament to the indomitable human spirit.

In tracing the intricate lines of rebellion, we confront the complexities of human history, where choices and circumstances intertwine to shape the fate of nations. It is a reminder that history is not just a collection of dates and events but a living, breathing entity that echoes through time, shaping the course of generations. As we explore this history, we are beckoned to confront uncomfortable truths, to challenge prevailing narratives, and to seek a deeper understanding of the human experience. The legacy of colonial rule is not merely a relic of the past but a living force that continues to shape the present, urging us to learn from the mistakes of the past and strive for a more just and equitable future.

The rebellion and its roots in the colonial past become

a mirror through which we reflect on our shared humanity, our capacity for both darkness and light. It calls upon us to acknowledge the wounds of history and endeavour to heal them, to forge a path towards reconciliation and peace. In the midst of this complex tapestry, the people of South Sudan continue to write their story, weaving threads of hope and resilience into the fabric of their nation's future. The rebellion is not just a footnote in history; it is an ongoing journey of transformation, a quest for justice, and a quest to shape their own destiny.

As we immerse ourselves in the rich narratives of rebellion, we are drawn into a world of paradoxes and contradictions, of sorrow and triumph. It is a world where the human spirit soars in the face of adversity, where the seeds of change are sown amidst the rubble of conflict.

And so, the analysis of the colonial rulers' legacy becomes more than just an academic exercise; it becomes an invitation to embrace the complexity of human history, to seek understanding and empathy, and to foster a shared commitment to build a better world, where the echoes of rebellion are replaced by the harmonies of peace. The entangled web of the British colonial legacy continued to weave its threads, now bearing witness to a momentous turn in 1946 when the Southern policy was abandoned, denounced as divisive by Northern elites (Mayo, 1994; Albino, 1970). While the apparent shift towards altruism may raise scepticism, deeper motives reveal the desire of Northerners to create captive populations in the South, subject to their dominance.

In their pursuit of self-determination, the Southern Sudanese stood at the precipice of history, their voices echoing across the land as they gathered at the momentous 1947 Juba Conference (Rahim, 1966). It was a gathering that bore the weight of their aspirations, a plea for protection from the looming spectre of repression that emanated from the North, where an Arab-Islamic elite held the reins of power. The Southern Sudanese yearned for a safeguard against the shadows of oppression, seeking solace in the embrace of a federated government system—a shield against the domination that threatened to engulf them. However, fate had other plans, and their heartfelt pleas fell on deaf ears, met with the cold rejection of Northern elites.

In the face of this disappointment, the Southern Sudanese found themselves at a crossroads, their dreams shattered but their spirit unyielding. It was at this juncture that the path of armed resistance beckoned; a path that would echo the timeless question posed by Tilly—what sets apart the violence of states from any other? Tilly's answer reverberated through the chronicles of history, revealing the enigmatic concept of 'legitimacy' (Tilly, 2003). It became a revelation, a key that unlocked the understanding of how countries like old Sudan were shaped by a complex interplay of intended and unintended effects, shaped by the colonial institutions that left an indelible mark on political order and authority.

The tapestry of Sudan's colonial past, intricate and finely woven, unfurled before us, a tableau of power dynamics, oppression, and resistance. It was a history that bore witness to the resilience of a people who refused to yield, who stood tall in the face of adversity, and who found strength in their collective struggle for justice and self-determination. As we trace the contours of this complex history, we come to recognize that the path to reconciliation and lasting peace lies in understanding the multifaceted tapestry of the past. It calls upon us to embrace empathy, to seek understanding in the midst of our differences, and to weave a collective journey towards a brighter and harmonious future.

The struggle of the Southern Sudanese is not just a tale of tribulations; it is a testament to the indomitable human spirit—the spirit that refuses to be cowed by the shadows of repression and oppression. It is a reminder that in the face of adversity, the human heart yearns for liberty and dignity, and the will to fight for a better tomorrow becomes an unyielding flame that illuminates the path ahead.

As we traverse this intricate tapestry of history, we are reminded that the quest for peace is not a solitary endeavour; it is a collective journey that binds us together as one human family. It beckons us to embrace our shared humanity, to stand in solidarity with one another, and to forge a future where the echoes of armed resistance are replaced by the harmonies of peace.

In the echoes of history, we find the resonance of hope—a hope that in understanding the past, we can pave the way for a future where justice, equality, and inclusivity reign. It is a journey of healing, of bridging divides, and of recognizing that our shared destiny is interwoven like the threads of a tapestry, forming a beautiful mosaic of unity amidst diversity.

Let us, then, be stewards of this intricate embroidery, cherishing its complexity, and weaving a future where the resilience of the Southern Sudanese becomes a beacon of inspiration for generations to come. In the unity of purpose and the pursuit of peace, we shall honour the struggles of the past and create a legacy that resonates with the timeless pursuit of humanity—for a world where the pursuit of self-determination is not an aspiration but a cherished reality.

CHAPTER 4

WAR & FAMINE

"Poverty is not an accident. Like slavery and apartheid, it is man-made and can be removed by the actions of human beings."

Nelson Mandela

The harrowing landscapes of war-torn South Sudan bear witness to the relentless force of poverty-induced violence, leaving behind a trail of destruction that scars the psychological, emotional, and physical well-being of its people. One haunting image that encapsulates the extent of the damage caused by war and famine is Kevin Carter's photograph "The Vulture and the Little Girl," taken in 1993 during the Sudanese famine, now known as South Sudan. In this heart-wrenching moment, a vulture lurks nearby, poised to feast on a starving child teetering on the brink of death. The child's emaciated state and the ominous presence of the vulture haunted Kevin Carter so deeply that he succumbed to depression and took his own life just three months after capturing this soul-crushing scene.

Kevin Carter, 1993

When I first encountered this photo at the age of 16, its impact seared itself into my memory, forever etching a deep sense of sorrow and empathy for my people enduring such immense suffering. This image captured a moment of devastation that mirrored the reality faced by countless children during the Sudanese war and the unforgiving grip of famine. Some of those who survived, against all odds, now walk among us as grown adults, while others have taken on the roles of parents. The true extent of what this war and violence have done to the people of Sudan and South Sudan is beyond any words that language can convey. The damage runs deep, the aftermath is haunting, and the current suffering endures as a profound testament to the lasting impact of such violence.

Kevin Carter's iconic photograph of the starving Sudanese girl and the vulture conveys a sense of suspended urgency, freezing a moment that teeters between hope and despair. The stillness of the child and the vulture pulsates with emotion, leaving viewers desperate for a second frame, a resolution to the haunting questions it poses. Within the realm of logic, only two possibilities exist: either the vulture feasted on the child, a grim fate that seemed inevitable at the moment of capture, or it did not. However, these possibilities transcend mere logical conclusions; they are laden with raw emotion, transforming into haunting questions that shake the foundations of our humanity. We are left questioning why violence and suffering persist, why natural and man-made disasters befall innocent souls, particularly the vulnerable and innocent, such as children.

In 1993, when the image was first published in The New York Times, the world turned to Kevin Carter, a South African photojournalist, seeking answers. The questions extended beyond the fate of the child to Carter's ethical stance. People questioned why he stood there taking pictures instead of rushing to aid the dying child. These questions soon turned into accusations, with some condemning Carter as another vulture, a predator preying on the scene of suffering. The answers to these questions and accusations lie within Carter's soon after decision to end his life.

This scary photograph continues to resonate with deep emotions and lingering queries, reflecting the complexities of human nature and the moral dilemmas that arise amidst tragedy. It forces us to confront uncomfortable truths about our society, the violence of war and poverty, and the toll it takes on the most vulnerable among us. The image serves as a haunting reminder of our collective responsibility to address the root causes of poverty and violence, to provide aid and support to those in need, and to strive for a world where such suffering becomes a distant memory.

Amidst the vast and intricate embroidery of Southern Sudan's famine lay a complex interplay of factors - civil war, famine, floods, drought, and disease - each thread weaving a tale of unimaginable suffering. Yet, in the collective consciousness of those who grew up in the '90s, that harrowing image of a starving child and the looming vulture came to symbolise not just a region but an entire continent's hunger, and the perceived indifference of photojournalists. The oft-repeated adage, "a picture is worth a thousand words," fuelled this attitude, and rightfully so, for images have the power to convey profound emotions and tell stories beyond words. However, there are moments when the depths of human suffering defy verbal expression, leaving us grasping for words that might never suffice.

The photographer behind this haunting image, Kevin

Carter, garnered recognition with the Pulitzer Prize in 1994, only to succumb to the weight of his own inner turmoil, committing suicide just three months later. For many, this tragic end seemed to confirm Carter's guilt and moral ambiguity. His post-Pulitzer statement, wherein he described lighting a cigarette, talking to God, and crying after capturing the photograph, only added to the perception of his insensitivity. However, those close to Carter knew that his pain stemmed not from the child in the photograph alone, but from the overwhelming suffering and death surrounding him as the violence and famine persisted. His preoccupation lay with what would become of all those starving and dying souls in wars zones wrapped in famine across the globe, not merely that one captured moment. Nevertheless, for distant onlookers, that singular question of the child's fate assumed greater importance, as it allowed them to contain their horror and outrage within that limited frame.

To those in the West, listening and watching from afar, Sudan appeared as a faraway land, distant and disconnected from their own realities. The sensations of days and days of hunger remained an abstract concept, something they assumed they were unlikely to experience. Bound within the constraints of that photograph, their questions extended, at most, to the person behind the camera. In doing so, they unwittingly transformed the child and the vulture's heart-wrenching tableau into an unfortunate accident, an isolated moment of fate. In their distant gaze, they questioned why Carter did not carry her to the feeding centre, as if he alone held the power to alter her fate. Yet, the reality was far more complex and multifaceted. Just as our current experiences in the west are complex.

Surrounded by the dire circumstances of famine, there would have been countless other suffering individuals around Carter, each in need of aid. Should he have carried them all? In essence, such a question misses the crux of the matter. The photographer's role extended beyond a singular act of heroism, and the burden of responsibility should not solely rest on one individual's shoulders. The tragedy and suffering depicted in that photograph were the result of a complex web of factors beyond one person's capacity to address – an understanding we need to apply when examining the role of violence and trauma within the South Sudanese and many other refugee migrant communities.

In truth, this haunting image serves as a profound reflection of humanity's collective struggle to comprehend and respond to the immense suffering and violence that plague various corners of the world. It questions our ability to empathize with distant horrors and underscores the need for broader societal awareness and action. Beyond that frame lies a broader narrative of human suffering, demanding our attention, empathy, and collective efforts to alleviate the violence of poverty and famine in all its dimensions.

Amidst the stark image of a starving child and a lurking vulture, there lies a hidden tapestry of violence, loss, and heartache that the photograph fails to capture. What eludes the viewer's gaze are the harrowing scenes of death, the brutal separation of families torn apart by the desire to stay together, the veterans and civilians left maimed by the horrors of war, and the mothers giving birth amidst flying bullets in the unforgiving wilderness. The young children, mere five and six years old, forcibly recruited into armies, and the child soldiers who, with their feeble arms, dug graves for their fallen comrades, are unseen and unheard. The elderly and children, too weak to keep walking to safety, dropping lifeless by the roadside due to the scarcity of resources caused by war and disaster - these complexities are the true causes behind the emaciated child in the photograph, and many others like her. The image, however, merely presents a glimpse of what those far removed from the reality of South Sudan/Sudanese or any war-torn land can comprehend and grapple with. It allows them to focus on elements they understand and can emotionally process, shielding them from the full depth of the horrors endured.

Similar to the heart-wrenching image of three-year-old Syrian Alan Kurdi's lifeless body washed ashore on a Turkish beach in 2015, these photographs serve as symbolic fragments of larger tragedies. Many three-year-olds continue to perish while crossing the treacherous Mediterranean Sea, but Kurdi's solitary figure lying face down on the beach made for a more poignant and dramatic image. Such visuals momentarily connect those in the West to distant sufferings, offering a sense of empathy without fully comprehending the true extent of the events unfolding elsewhere.

The questions we ask and where we choose to direct our focus determine the actions we take in response to these visual triggers. Should our gaze remain fixed on the vulture, we might seek answers from the photographer, Kevin Carter. Yet, if we shift our focus to the child's hunger - the central protagonist of the image - we would demand answers from the government and all actors playing a role in global wars and famine that actively contributed to Southern Sudan's famine in 1993. Carter's lens captured a reality so distressing that it plunged him into a deep depression, eventually leading to his untimely demise. One can only begin to imagine the unimaginable pain, suffering, and untreated emotional, mental, and physical wounds endured by those who were born and raised amidst the relentless turmoil.

Indeed, the photograph serves as a mere fragment of the vast mosaic of suffering etched into the lives of countless South Sudanese and those affected by war and disaster. The pain is palpable, the scars deep, and the cries for help echo through the ages. The narrative of anguish, resilience, and hope unfolds beyond the confines of that single frame, waiting to be truly understood, felt, and addressed with the urgency and compassion it so rightly deserves.

This photo, vividly depicting the real face of untold, yet preventable suffering, weighed so heavily on Kevin Carter, despite his accolades. It ultimately led to his demise, exacerbating several challenges he faced. If Kevin Carter, through his lens, could fall into a deep depression, driving him to an early grave, how much more pain must the South Sudanese, the real victims, have endured? How immense must their pain, their suffering, their deep untreated emotional, mental, and physical wounds be?

In the depths of Kevin Carter's soul, a haunting darkness cast its shadow, an unyielding weight that bore down upon him like an unforgiving burden. The very photograph he had captured, frozen in time, became an indelible mark on his psyche, etching its presence in the deepest recesses of his mind. It was an image that transcended the realms of the visual, seeping into the realm of emotion, tormenting him with its relentless power. "I am haunted," his poignant suicide note read, and in those few words, he revealed the depth of his internal struggle. The haunting memories of the horrors he had witnessed through his lens clung to him like spectral apparitions, replaying themselves in an endless loop within his troubled mind. The weight of the world seemed to rest upon his weary shoulders, as he battled not just his own personal demons but also the harrowing scenes of killings, corpses, and suffering that he had captured. The trauma he had witnessed and secondary acquired had woven itself into the fabric of his being, leaving him emotionally scarred and psychologically burdened.

Haunted by the stark reality of starvation, wounded children, trigger-happy madmen, and the anguish of violence, he found himself trapped in a perpetual maze of pain and despair. The anguish of these haunting visions seemed to echo endlessly within his soul, a symphony of sorrow that drowned out any glimmer of hope. The financial woes he faced only added to the weight of his burden. The demands of life pressed upon him, squeezing the breath from his lungs like a tightening noose. The absence of a phone, the lack of money for rent, child support, and debts, created an unyielding sense of desperation, amplifying the shadows that loomed over him.

In the midst of his struggle, he longed to find solace and refuge, seeking the company of a fellow soul, Ken, in the after-life. The weight of his own pain and the collective pain of those he had captured through his lens became an unbearable yoke, driving him to seek an escape from the relentless haunting. In the end, the burden became too much to bear, and he surren-dered to the darkness that had pursued him relentlessly. His choice to depart from this world was not just an escape from financial hardships but an attempt to find release from the relentless haunting of his own photographs, a desperate bid to lay down the burden he had carried for far too long. The photo-graph that had once earned him the prestigious Pulitzer Prize now stood as a sombre reminder of the toll his chosen path had taken. Kevin Carter, a photojournalist whose lens had exposed the world's pain, had ultimately become a victim of the very pain he had sought to expose. We then need to ask ourselves when we are tempted to judge, punish or to turn a blind eye to the behaviours and perpetration of violence possibly as a result of inner turmoil in the South Sudanese communities – if a witness such as Carter who suffered a second degree trauma could struggle to live after his experience in South Sudan/Sudan, then what does that imply for the actual people who were the victims of these inhumane, violent experiences – the South Sudanese people.

His suicide note spoke volumes about the depths of his torment, a testament to the haunting nature of the visual stories he had captured. It is a stark reminder of the tremendous emotional toll that witnessing and documenting human suffering can take on those who bear witness.

His suicide note read:

> *"I am depressed . . . without phone . . . money for rent . . . money for child support . . . money for debts . . . money!!! . . . I am haunted by the vivid memories of killings & corpses & anger & pain . . . of starving or wounded children, of trigger-happy madmen, often police, of killer executioners. I have gone to join Ken if I am that lucky."*
>
> **- Kevin Carter, 1994**

We then need to ask ourselves, especially those who work in the social and criminal justice system, whether many of the so-called criminal offences committed by South Sudanese individuals are rooted in inherent criminality, a predisposition towards criminal behaviour, or if there are significant factors to consider regarding their psychological states and the profound traumas they have experienced, coupled with existing social inequalities.

CHAPTER 5

"OUR MINDS
ARE DAMAGED"
SUFFERING LEFT
US TRAUMATISED

"In the rush of life, I find myself reaching out to grasp the air, a reminder that I am still here, breathing, but sometimes feeling disconnected from the essence of true living. What is life, I wonder? Is it merely a biological process of consuming air to stay conscious, or is there something more profound that eludes me? As a disabled veteran on the roadside, I contemplate the enigma of existence, yearning for a sense of purpose and meaning beyond the scars

and wounds I carry. Amidst the cosmic dance of questions and seeking, I embrace nature's solace, hoping to truly thrive and be alive, finding solace in the poetry of my own existence and the survival of my soul.

- Veteran

During the early 2022 visit, the vibrant pulse of South Sudan beckoned, and I found myself gathered with an eclectic group of friends and acquaintances for a lunch outing. Among us were a few men and two gracious ladies, each bringing a diverse range of experiences and professions to the table. Lawyers and academics lent their intellectual fervour, while a youth pastor exuded a sense of compassion and guidance. Accompanying them were shrewd businessmen, their minds attuned to the intricacies of commerce and trade. In the midst of this motley crew, the stage was set for an engaging and enlightening conversation as we enjoyed a delicious meal.

In the midst of animated conversation, the atmosphere seemed charged with unspoken sorrows and simmering tensions, like a tempest brewing beneath a serene facade. As the sun dipped below the horizon, casting its warm hues across the gathering, the storyteller's words wove a tapestry of heartbreak and resilience. The tales told of a nation, South Sudan, where the echoes of war had carved deep chasms in the souls of its people.

In the eyes of the lawyers and academics, one could glimpse the passion of advocates seeking justice, their voices rising and falling like waves crashing against the shores of injustice. Their debates danced like flickering flames, illuminating the dark corners of the nation's collective trauma. And there, seated among them, the youth pastor exuded a profound sense of duty, as if carrying the burden of healing a nation's wounded spirit.

But it was the businessman who drew on the power of parables and humour to drive home a profound truth. With a twinkle in his eye, he asked, "What is this relentless ghost haunting our hearts, like a spectre we cannot shake off?" His seemingly simple diagnostic test—born of South Sudanese parents or on South Sudanese soil—revealed a truth hidden in plain sight. The scars of war, like ancestral shadows, traversed generations, whispering secrets of pain and loss.

In that moment, the stories of sorrow and violence merged with the laughter of camaraderie, forming an intricate mosaic of a people who had known both great triumph and unspeakable tragedy. As the night wore on, the stars above seemed to bear witness to the weight of the past, their twinkling light a testament to the resilience of the human spirit.

The young woman's account of unspeakable horrors lingered in the air, like an elusive mist that left hearts heavy with the burden of understanding. A land once torn apart by conflict now grappled with a new adversary—the intergenerational cycle of violence. As the group pondered the complexities of trauma, the boundaries between personal and interpersonal violence blurred, revealing the interconnectedness of their shared struggles.

Amidst the animated discourse, one could sense the yearning for divine intervention, a longing for healing that transcended the confines of the material world. The businessman inquired, "Can prayer alone mend these wounds, or do we need the wisdom of healers and therapists to guide us through the labyrinth of trauma?" Like a chorus of prayers whispered into the night, the hope for reconciliation and redemption echoed through the hearts of those present. As the moon cast its gentle glow upon the gathering, illuminating the faces of those bound by a shared heritage, it became clear that South Sudan's path to healing would require a tapestry of more than just prayers and economically improved situation as the business put it. The wounds of war were not merely physical but spiritual, etched into the very fabric of the nation's identity, the pastor believes. The country needs research-based approaches for trauma repair and recovery, said, the academic.

In that moment, beneath the starlit sky, the conversation transcended the boundaries of time and space. The stories of South Sudan's past, present, and future intertwined, forming a needlepoint of resilience, courage, and hope. The youth pastor asked, "Can we break free from the chains of trauma and create a new legacy for the generations to come?" As the night drew to a close, a profound sense of interconnectedness lingered, uniting the voices in a collective call for healing, justice, and lasting peace.

The businessman's two questions hung in the air like an unyielding riddle, probing the depths of our souls with their profound simplicity. "Are you South Sudanese by birth? Were you born of South Sudanese parents? If your answers are yes to both questions, then you are traumatised." He delivered his diagnostic test with a mix of seriousness and humour, but beneath our laughter, we sensed the weight of truth in his words. As we observed the turmoil in our homeland and the struggles within South Sudanese families abroad, we could discern the echoes of generational and intergenerational trauma reverberating within us.

His method, though unorthodox, carried a profound insight—a glimpse into the tangled web of traumas passed down through the generations. These wounds, like haunting ghosts, had refused to dissipate even after the guns fell silent and independence was won. Instead, they persisted, haunting our lives and manifesting in the most destructive ways, often manifesting in violence—be it personal or interpersonal. No psychiatrist was needed to discern the deep scars etched into the collective psyche of our people. The anguish and pain were palpable, woven into the very fabric of our existence. The trauma of war, loss, displacement, settlement in unfamiliar lands where we are often not so welcome had seeped into our souls, shaping our responses and behaviours, often leading to a cycle of violence that seemed impossible to break.

In his seemingly simplistic approach, the businessman had stumbled upon a universal truth—the trauma we carried within us had become an indelible part of our identity. It was engraved in the lines of our faces, the sorrow in our eyes, and the heaviness in our hearts. The wounds of the past had left an indelible mark, passed down from one generation to the next like an unwelcome inheritance, whether we recognise it or not. As we grappled with the consequences of this inherited pain, we realised that healing was not a matter of mere time or wishful thinking. It required a collective effort—a reckoning with our past, an acknowledgment of our shared struggles, and a commitment to breaking free from the chains of trauma. Only then could we begin to build a brighter future for ourselves and the generations to come.

The businessman's unconventional diagnosis had sparked a profound conversation among us, unearthing emotions long buried and questions left unanswered. It was a moment of soul-searching, a collective journey into the depths of our shared trauma, and a realization that healing would require more than just time—it demanded a courageous confrontation of our past and a determined march toward a better tomorrow.

The chilling darkness of violence cast its haunting shadow upon South Sudan, a land marred by the frequency of human loss, both through interpersonal brutality and the grim spectre of so-called judicial executions. Among the myriad inhumane cases that echo through the nation's history, one instance stands out, leaving the country horrified in 2018—the extrajudicial killing of Gatluak Majok Liey, Nyuon Garang Kuol, Pur Ruop Kuol, and Dhoal Barpuoh Tap. These four young men fell victim to a barbaric act of terror allegedly ordered by Unity State governors.

On that fateful Monday in August, social media became a stage for the world to witness the depths of cruelty unleashed upon these victims in Unity State, South Sudan. The incident was described as a revenge killing for the deaths of eight civilians. The suspects were apprehended in the neighbouring Kordofan State in Sudan and handed over to the Unity State government for further investigation, but tragically, they faced a public execution that shocked the world. Those who witnessed this killing were left in horror across the globe.

Amidst the horror and sorrow, questions lingered about who had sanctioned the heinous act. Unity State Governor and the Presidential Advisor on Security were suspected to have had a hand in blessing the execution. The exchange between Gatluak Majok Liey, the suspect, and the South Sudan People's Defence Forces (SSPDF) soldiers before they set him ablaze sent shivers down the spines of those who bore witness to the video recording posted and widely shared on social media platforms such as myself.

The incident shed light on the broader context of violence in South Sudan, a nation scarred by intense conflict during and after the civil war. Unity State bore the brunt of this violence, witnessing a series of extrajudicial killings and gross human rights violations. From 2014 to 2017, innocent lives, including those of children and the elderly, were lost in appalling acts of brutality, including firing squads, burning people alive in tukuls, and mutilating body parts. The social-cultural complexities in South Sudan further fuelled this cycle of violence, as families and clans found themselves pitted against each other in feuds and endless conflicts.

Despite international condemnation and the notion of accountability being integrated into the Revitalized Peace

Agreement, those responsible for these heinous acts were yet to face justice. The recorded execution of Gatluak Majok Liey and his companions stands as a harrowing testament to the depths of brutality unleashed upon the people of South Sudan. The horrific events of August 8, 2022, which will discuss as a case study were captured on film and circulated through social media, exposing the world to the grim reality faced by these victims. Gatluak Majok Liey was burned alive in a small hut, while the three others met their fate through a firing squad, a chilling manifestation of the violence that has plagued the nation for years.

Bound by chains on both ankles and arms, Gatluak Majok's unwavering resolve defied the impending capital punishment looming before him, seemingly a vengeful retribution for the late brother of one of the ministers. In a remarkable display of courage, he addressed his killers with calm assurance, declaring that even without the chains, he would never flee from his fate. With the weight of imminent death upon him, Gatluak began by offering well wishes to the country, a poignant gesture in the face of his own mortality. Yet, his final words were laced with a chilling warning to his executors—to remain vigilant, for his comrades would seek revenge. In the midst of his speech, Gatluak's countenance remained resolute, displaying no hint of fear or plea for mercy. Instead, a smile graced his lips, and laughter bubbled forth as he answered his executors with unshakeable composure. The following haunting phrases exchanged between him and the South Sudan People's Defence Forces (SSPDF) soldiers reverberated through the hearts of those present, leaving an indelible impression of a man unyielding in the face of an inevitable and gruesome fate.

Their conversation on the scene of execution as follows:

GATLUAK: I don't have any problem; I just wish you to remain in peace but please protect our country. You the youth do not allow the elders to freely misbehave, declare war and fight them if necessary.

SSPDF Soldier: "Stop lying."

GATLUAK: Yes, "you can deny it because you have been bribed but I know you will come to your senses once the money paid to bribe you is over."

SSPDF Soldier: "Can I tie the handcuff together with the rope—"

SSPDF Soldier: "Yes, because the handcuff will not be burnt, please you tie both legs."

GATLUAK: "You guys just use the ropes to tie me, the handcuff will help you during your operation."

SSPDF Soldier: "No, we have plenty of them."

GATLUAK: "You stop this madness. I will not run away. the whole of me Gatluak to run, no!"

SSPDF Soldier: "Why are you talking too much? Chidong, what are you doing with that rope?"

GATLUAK: "Allows him to bring it so that he can tie it to my left leg. Why do you act like jinja beer my friend Gatnyatuoroaah?"

SSPDF Soldier: "Am very annoyed, the men you have killed from our clan are really great men."

GATLUAK: "But you are pointing at me. Is this revenge or are you acting in your capacity as a soldier implementing government directives? If it is a government directive Mr. Wicgoal cannot finger point me."

SSPDF Soldier: "Stop this nonsense of talking about your strong men, if I got you that day you would be dead by now."

SSPDF (Mr. Wichgoal): "If I was there, I would not move in that car, it was just because I came in a plane, I would have searched for you because I know you are hiding in those bushes, we would have fought seriously."

GATLUAK: "Look how difficult it is to arrest Gatluak Majiok, you can compare the scenario of my arrest to the arrest of Gatluak Manguel. You see how you are panicking. Please be vigilant, the bushes are full of my guys. they will finish you one by one."

SSPDF Soldier: "You are lying."

GATLUAK: "Who is that standing at the door side like some-one who has polluted? Are you Gatnyatuoroaah?"

In the annals of South Sudan's history, amidst the harrowing tales of countless gruesome killings, one particular incident stands as a haunting example of the dark depths to which violence can plunge humanity. The victims, in the face of their imminent demise, bore a chilling demeanour of honour, a reflection of the deeply ingrained mentality forged by years of civil war, where the act of killing and being killed had been tragically normalized. Like a perverse symphony, these tragic events orchestrated a crescendo of suffering for the Nuer community, echoing the relentless violation of basic human rights, where politicians and officers employed policies that inflicted pain upon innocent citizens in the name of warfare.

In the midst of such horrors, my attempt to comprehend the inexplicable began to take root. It was a compelling quest to decipher the cause behind an act of violence so extreme, pushing beyond the boundaries of physical reality and chal-lenging the very essence of our humanity. The brutality of these killings, akin to ripping an unborn child from its mother's womb and butchering it alongside her in the 2013 conflict, along with the so-called "judicial executions" of four soldiers, ignited a profound search within me. Such violence demon-strated the utter loss of the very essence that defines us as humans—the sacred threads of compassion and empathy that constitute our collective "humanity." These unspeakable acts tore at the very fabric of human existence, leaving us to question what years of war, famine, violence, and hardship could do to the human soul.

The soldiers, perpetrators of this barbaric violence, whether acting under superior orders or driven by their own deeply ingrained consciousness of violence, stand as both villains and victims in this tragic tale. A culture steeped in the stark reality of "kill or be killed" forces us to confront fundamental questions about humanity, guilt, remorse, and the humanity of those who carry out such acts, as well as the suffering of the victims and their loved ones. Are these soldiers themselves not "dead but not buried"? Their emotional and psychological well-being ravaged beyond repair by the scars of war, they seemingly lose their connection to humanity and the value of human life—a right to a fair trial now an unreachable concept. As we peer into the minds of these soldiers and the civilians caught in the crossfire, another heart-rending question arises: How can we transcend hatred in a land and among people where violent conflict has shattered the very essence of humanity's fabric? For those entwined in the same society as their oppressors, turning a blind eye to this inquiry is not an option.

Opening ourselves to critically analyse what lies beneath the eyes becomes a vital step towards redefining our perception of such barbaric acts, recognizing that evil, much like a sinister spectre, can emerge from the darkest shadows of any political system born from a history of violence. Throughout history, oppressive regimes have transformed into oppressors themselves, revealing the profound complexities that underlie what we label as "evil." The violators of human rights, when vulnerable and exposed, present an opportunity for others to witness them as fellow human beings. Such encounters raise a poignant question: Can they still embrace their humanity and share a moment of empathy with those whose lives they have shattered with trauma and misery? The families of these victims. This predicament invokes Hannah Arendt's phrase, "the banality of evil," a concept that attempts to fathom the intricacies of what constitutes true malevolence.

Encountering those who once engineered state-sponsored atrocities may offer invaluable insights into the making of "monsters" within a political system that employs repressive violence to achieve its ends. By delving into the heart of darkness and facing these architects of evil, perhaps we can hope to shed light on the path to redemption and a future where violence is a relic of the past.

In the end, the journey toward healing, understanding, reconciliation, and fairness may not be smooth, but it remains essential. As we navigate through the ruins of a turbulent past, seeking a collective transformation, let us not forget that the human soul has the capacity to rebuild itself from the ashes of devastation. Only then can we begin to dream of a South Sudan where the scars of violence have healed, and the fabric of humanity is rewoven with threads of compassion and peace.

In the labyrinth of understanding the minds of those who commit unspeakable acts of evil, we encounter a disquieting paradox. It is a perilous journey, one that we must undertake to fully grasp the genesis and sustenance of violence in places like South Sudan, where the echoes of history and the current turmoil intertwine in a haunting dance. Christopher Browning's meticulous study of the men embroiled in the tragic Holocaust (2017) sheds light on the idea that understanding demands a courageous attempt at empathy. Nevertheless, he vehemently dismisses the notion that explanation equates to exoneration or that comprehension equates to absolution. The question looms before us like a riddle cloaked in shadows: To what extent does seeking understanding blur the line between explanation and pardon, and does it inadvertently grant clemency to the perpetrators?

This question of "understanding" those who perpetrate extreme acts of violence has ignited fierce debates, leading some to assert that those responsible for unfathomable atrocities are not worthy of scrutiny from scholars and seekers of truth. Emile Fackenheim's (1989) enigmatic notion of a "double move" captures the intricate dance between seeking explanation and resisting the allure of pardon. As we grapple with the coexistence of good and evil within human souls, we confront the tumultuous interplay of tensions and complexities that this paradox presents. To resist the seductive charms of evasive explanations or empty consolation becomes the true test of our intellectual and moral fortitude. Some may argue that delving into the realm of understanding evil is tantamount to treading on violated ground, an act of committing an "obscenity."

The violent history and present turmoil in South Sudan bear witness to the profound struggles with violence that have become deeply personal. Within the hearts of these soldiers, a complex tapestry of violence unfolds, defying simplistic labels such as "killers." When nations send their sons and daughters to war, the conflict all too often engulfs their spirits, leaving many shattered upon their return. The wounds borne by these warriors cut deeper than flesh, searing their souls with emotional torment. As the philosopher Edmund Burke once opined, those crushed by oppressive laws often become the enemies of the very system that oppresses them. A nation caught in the clutches of trauma must grapple with the deeper issues plaguing its society and its people if it is to break free from the vicious cycle of violence and the repetitive churn of leadership.

As we traverse the highway of time, signposts of "yesterday" emerge at every mile, reminding us of the inescapable past. Life, in its quest to cleanse itself of historical burdens, may unleash unexplained physical reactions, a tempest of emotions disproportionate to the trigger. Trauma not only ruptures relationships but distorts our perceptions, casting our view of the world through fragmented prisms of our past. To perceive ourselves and our world more clearly, we yearn for resonance and relation with others, just as an infant craves its mother's empathetic embrace to perceive and explore its world.

Collective cultural traumas breed misunderstandings and stereotypes that echo through the collective consciousness. Societal perceptions become imbued with limiting beliefs and unconscious codes, obscuring our sense of togetherness and preventing the synchronicity of harmonious collaboration.

Our vital inner compass falters, unable to receive the energy and information necessary to chart a path of collective growth.

In the tragic tapestry of violence, seeking reparations and healing after the irrevocable damage is akin to a futile whisper in the tempestuous winds. Prevention stands as the beacon of hope, a light we must zealously pursue. By delving deep into the enigma of why individuals resort to violence, whether against others or themselves, we can fortify our defences against the tides of destruction before they surge beyond the point of no return. Vigilant understanding grants us the tools to intervene promptly, vigorously, and with purpose.

In this ever-evolving odyssey of comprehension, we must navigate the turbulent waters of human nature, embracing the complexity and darkness within us. For it is only through seeking true understanding and confronting the shades of our shared humanity that we can inch closer to the elusive shores of peace and redemption.

In the tapestry of human suffering, the threads of explicit and implicit harm intertwine to create a complex and haunting mosaic. Each act of violence leaves its mark, a stark stroke of pain and devastation etched upon the canvas of existence. In the immediate aftermath of a criminal act, the explicit suffering is painfully evident, like a crimson stain upon the soul of the victim. But the true extent of the damage goes beyond the visible wounds, seeping into the very essence of the individual and their community.

The trauma's tendrils are insidious, extending far beyond the present moment. Over time, the reverberations of agony spread like ripples in a still pond, affecting not only the victims but also their loved ones and future generations. This transgenerational trauma echoes through the ages, like a haunting melody that cannot be silenced. It finds expression in the communities where history's scars still linger, where the pain of colonisation and other past violence has left an indelible mark on the people's collective psyche. Substance abuse and violence become visible manifestations of this unhealed anguish, like shadows cast by the weight of history's burden (Atkinson, 2002).

Amidst the sea of suffering, explicit traumas disrupt the lives of individuals, leaving them adrift in a tempest of pain. The wounds inflicted upon their spirits impede growth, hindering the flow of life's currents. Yet, these individual tragedies are but droplets in the vast ocean of collective trauma. The waves of shared anguish create an intricate embroidery of pain that weaves its way through cultures and societies. Like an ancient tapestry, it bears the imprint of untold stories, of silenced grief, and unresolved memories. The culture itself becomes a vessel of unhealed wounds, carrying the echoes of the past into the present (Atkinson, 2002).

Breaking free from this cycle of suffering requires a revival of thought and a cultural revolution. The structures that perpetuate these hurts and sufferings must be dismantled, brick by brick, until the foundations of healing are firmly laid. It is a quest for transformation - not just of external systems but of internal paradigms - a journey that calls for introspection and collective action. Only through this transformative process can the shackles of trauma be broken, and the spirit of the community set free to soar once more.

In the labyrinth of trauma's aftermath, the quest for truth becomes a lifeline for healing and restoration. Yet, this journey is fraught with conflicts and contradictions, like an intricate dance between light and shadow. The survivors of atrocities carry their stories like sacred relics, but their retelling may be fragmented and tumultuous. In these chaotic narratives lies the essence of truth - a truth that some forces seek to suppress. The battle between denial and proclamation becomes the heart of psychological trauma, and the stories of those who have suffered are often dismissed or doubted. But it is only when the truth is brought into the open, when the voices of survivors are finally heard and believed, that the healing process can begin (Herman, 1997; 2015).

Yet, the path to truth is fraught with obstacles. Secrecy and darkness may shroud the traumatic events, preventing them from being expressed as clear and coherent narratives. Instead, they surface as symptoms, like enigmatic riddles that haunt the community's consciousness. The scars of unspoken suffering are etched upon the collective psyche, leaving wounds that may not easily heal. The journey toward healing and societal restoration requires a commitment to transparency and an unwavering dedication to unveiling the buried truths. It is a pilgrimage of courage and compassion, where the scars of the past are not hidden but embraced, in the pursuit of a brighter future (Atkinson, 2002; Herman, 1997).

In the symphony of human suffering and redemption,

empathy takes centre stage as the conductor, and humanity itself forms the orchestra. As we delve into the depths of trauma and seek to understand its intricate layers, we must be guided by the unwavering light of compassion and the profound wisdom of solidarity. Our journey is not one of simple and quick resolutions but a profound and essential exploration of the very essence of our shared humanity.

In this expedition through the dark recesses of trauma, we must embrace the power of truth, compassion, and resilience. Each note played in this symphony represents the stories of countless individuals who have endured pain, loss, and despair. As we listen to their melodies, we must respond with empathy, acknowledging the weight of their experiences and the validity of their emotions.

The orchestra of humanity is comprised of diverse voices, each with its unique struggles and triumphs. In this grand composition, we must harmonise our collective efforts to create a space of healing and understanding. Our shared humanity binds us together, and in recognising the interconnectedness of our experiences, we can find solace in knowing that we are not alone in our struggles.

Through the power of compassion, we extend a hand to those who have suffered, reaching across the chasms of pain and sorrow to offer support and comfort. It is through this deep connection that we can begin to mend the broken pieces of the human soul and stitch together the threads of hope for a much-healed and brighter future.

The journey towards repair is not one taken alone; it is a

joint endeavour where survivors, their communities, national decision-makers, politicians, and those in positions that affect change walk hand in hand. As we navigate the complexities of trauma and its aftermath, we must remember that healing is not solely an individual process but a collective transformation of the human spirit. Drawing inspiration from the words of Atkinson (2002) and Herman (1997), we understand that the road to healing is paved with the courage to confront the past, the strength to face the pain, and the willingness to embrace vulnerability. It is in this embrace of our shared humanity, flaws and all, that we find the seeds of redemption and renewal.

As the symphony plays on, we find ourselves entangled in the intricacies of human experience. Yet, amid the dissonance and harmony, we discover the universal thread that binds us together—the capacity to empathise, to understand, and to heal. With every note played and every beat of the collective heart, we move closer to a future where trauma does not define us but becomes a catalyst for growth and resilience. It is through the transformative power of compassion that we can elevate ourselves beyond the confines of suffering and embrace the fullness of our shared humanity.

In this symphony of suffering and redemption, may we, as a united humanity, stand as witnesses to the stories of survival and the triumph of the human spirit. And may the conductor of empathy guide us towards a crescendo of healing—a symphony that resonates not only within the individual survivors but also within the collective soul of humanity itself.

CHAPTER 6

COMMUNITY VIOLENCE

"With lateral violence, the oppressed become the oppressors. We've internalised the pain of colonisation and our oppression and we've taken it into our communities."

- Allen Benson

Amidst the euphoria of political and geographical independence in Sudan and South Sudan, a shadow continues to linger—a haunting legacy that refuses to fade away. Colonial violence, like a relentless spectre, has manifested itself through the ages, birthing a new form of turmoil—community violence. Community violence happens between unrelated individuals, who may or may not know each other, generally outside the home, in a community or communal settings. Examples include assaults or fights among groups and shootings in public places, such as schools and on the streets. Research indicates that youth and young adults (ages 10-34), particularly those in communities of colour, are disproportionately impacted.

As we cast our gaze upon the civil unrest in South Sudan in 2013 and the military Faust in Sudan in 2023, we are confronted with the painful truth that independence from colonisation does not guarantee freedom from violence (Human Rights Watch, 2021). The intertwined roots of colonisation, war, border violence experienced through migration, and community violence run deep, for one has sown the seeds of the other, entwining their destinies in a macabre dance.

In the heart of South Sudan's tumultuous journey to nationhood, a sinister force lurked within, one that tore at the very fabric of unity—the spectre of community violence. Often associated with toxic behaviours within one's community, this insidious form of conflict took on a new guise in the context of the nation's birth. It is the violence that arose from within, a conflict perpetuated among ourselves, by ourselves.

As we trace the historical footsteps of South Sudan, we encounter the dark legacy of lateral violence, a force that wielded its destructive power during a crucial chapter of the nation's history. In the face of a quest for identity and autonomy, the once united people found themselves divided along ethno-regional lines, as Northerners clashed with Southerners, tribes against tribes, and clan against clan in the South, sowing seeds of discord and paving the path towards a catastrophic civil war.

The theory behind community violence explains that this behaviour is often the result of disadvantage, discrimination, and oppression, and that it arises from working within a society that is not designed for our way of doing things (Australian Human Rights Commission, 2011).

The consequences of the 2013 civil war were dire, as South Sudan became ensnared in a relentless cycle of violence that left scars etched deep into the nation's soul. Decades of bloodshed, pain, and anguish unfolded, culminating in the eventual partition of the land into two separate entities—South Sudan and Sudan. Yet, even after this division, community violence refused to abate, its sinister strands reaching far beyond political boundaries. Within our communities, community violence continues to wield its destructive influence, intertwining with the violence imposed upon us by external forces and perpetuated through entrenched systems. The wounds inflicted by ethno-regional conflicts are further exacerbated by the strife that brews among our own people, as we grapple with politically and ethnically deep-rooted grievances compounded by social and economic injustices.

At times, it may seem that the enemy lies outside, as we point fingers and cast blame upon external forces. However, in truth, as well as we struggle to make sense of external perpetrators, we must confront the shadows within—the community violence that festers and fractures our collective unity. It is a reflection of our own unresolved conflicts, the interplay of fear, envy, and resentment that prevents us from achieving true reconciliation and progress.

To break free from this destructive cycle, we must cultivate a culture of understanding, empathy, healing, and equal distribution of resources among ourselves. Acknowledging the role of community violence is not a declaration of weakness but rather an acknowledgement of what is broken in order to repair it. By facing our internal conflicts, we open the door to healing and reconciliation, creating a space where genuine dialogue and understanding can take root.

As we traverse the labyrinthine path of South Sudan's history, we are called upon to challenge the ghosts of community violence that continue to haunt our communities in the diaspora. It requires a collective effort, a commitment to foster an environment where diverse perspectives can coexist in harmony, and where the scars of the past can be transformed into a source of collective resilience and strength.

In the pages that lie ahead, we shall confront the complexities of community violence, recognising its destructive impact on our journey as people and of the nation of South Sudan. My mission here is not to assign blame but to unveil the underlying dynamics, to dissect the web of grievances, and to seek the path towards preventative measures and healing. Only by acknowledging and addressing lateral violence can we pave the way for South Sudanese that stands united, with a shared vision of peace and prosperity for all its people.

The echoes of trauma and disconnection reverberate through the corridors of time, seeping into the fabric of South Sudanese communities. In moments of anger, hurt, and powerlessness, the burden is sometimes too great to bear, and the frustration finds an outlet closer to home. This phenomenon is known as 'community violence,' a sideways eruption of emotions and grievances onto those within reach. South Sudanese undermine each other, creating divisions within their communities, leaving scars that run deep and wounds that are slow to heal.

Trapped within the margins of society, community violence often takes root among the oppressed themselves. The weight of oppression and the burden of intergenerational trauma and socio-economic challenges create a toxic cocktail, turning the oppressed into oppressors of the 'weak' among themselves, locked in a vicious cycle of abuse. The chains of community violence find their origins in the harrowing history of colonisation, civil war, oppression, and the enduring experiences of social and criminal injustice, intertwined with the brambles of socio-economic disadvantage.

In the heart of South Sudan and within its diaspora, community violence has become a learned pattern, etched across generations—a poignant social problem that demands our collective attention and introspection. It is a twisted vine that threatens to entangle the roots of unity and progress, requiring a concerted effort to untangle the knots of division and animosity. The road to reconciliation lies in acknowledging the scars of history, the wounds of the present, and the collective responsibility to break the chains of lateral violence that bind us.

To address community violence, we must sow the seeds understanding what is happening to us, for us and within us, and compassion and the need for repair, for within this complex tapestry of trauma and societal strife lies the potential for healing and transformation. Just as community violence is a cycle born from internal struggles, so too can the cycle be broken by the strength of our collective will. It is a paradox—a moment of both vulnerability and empowerment—as we confront the shadows within and forge a path towards harmony and unity.

As the journey unfolds, we must ask ourselves the riddle of reconciliation: How do we mend the fractures within our communities without perpetuating the cycle of violence? The answer lies not in further division but in collective introspection, in holding hands and hearts, and in recognizing that our destinies are intertwined like the threads of a tapestry. It is in understanding that community violence is not just an individual affliction but a communal discontent that demands a collective remedy.

To unravel the intricate web of community violence trauma, we must don the cloak of empathy, seeking to understand the pain and struggles of our fellow South Sudanese. In this shared quest for healing, establishing social and psychological services, we shall weave a new narrative—a tapestry of compassion and resilience that transcends the boundaries of time and history. It is through the transformation of unity that we shall forge a future where community violence is but a distant memory—a relic of a bygone era. As we journey towards the horizon of peace and unity, let us remember that our strength lies not in division but in the power of reconciliation and solidarity.

In the symphony of our collective efforts, we shall birth a

dawn where the shadows of community violence are cast aside, and the rays of peace illuminate our path. It is a journey that calls for courage, for it is only by facing our demons that we can conquer them. As we embark on this odyssey of healing, let us embrace the paradoxical truth that it is in the depths of vulnerability that we find the wellspring of strength—a strength that shall guide us towards a brighter tomorrow, united in purpose, and resolute in our commitment for a community where community violence is but a distant echo.

Community violence, like a festering wound, lingers through generations, placing immense pressure on kinship networks and shattering relationships. Its insidious effects can leave individuals feeling reluctant to assume leadership positions, insecure in their identities, and disconnected from their sources of strength and belonging. In moments of powerlessness and frustration, people may inadvertently resort to wielding power over others in destructive ways, perpetuating the cycle of violence. As we have long witnessed in colonised nations, displaced violence becomes the unfortunate legacy of colonisation and oppression, where anger and rage find a tragic outlet within oppressed communities. Instead of confronting the true oppressors, individuals turn against their own peers, their very own brothers and sisters. In First Nations communities across the globe, the scars of colonisation manifest in community violence, a heart-wrenching cycle of self-inflicted harm. South Sudanese, too, bear witness to this unfortunate phenomenon, with community violence manifested in the form of youth violence, family and domestic violence, gang conflicts, and divisive behaviour based on tribal affiliations. The transmission of community violence, intergenerational in nature, perpetuates the trauma within South Sudanese communities. Like a shadow cast upon the land, the consequences of community violence continue to be felt through the ages, sowing discord and disunity among our people.

In February 2022, I embarked on a journey to South Sudan, a land steeped in history and memories of my late father. I travelled with a friend, who initially seemed hesitant to join me on this pilgrimage. A battle of words ensued, but beneath the surface, I sensed her fear and uncertainty about returning to the land of our ancestors. Her stubborn facade, a mask she often wore during disagreements, began to crack, revealing glimpses of vulnerability and apprehension. I decided to bide my time, knowing that convincing her required a delicate approach. As the night unfolded, I engaged in a candid conversation with her, seeking to understand her deepest concerns. Her resistance stemmed not from stubbornness but from genuine fear. She feared the unknown that awaited her in South Sudan and the memories that may resurface upon setting foot in the land of our heritage.

Ultimately, I made the decision to proceed with my journey, leaving her in Nairobi, her place of refuge. As I arrived in Juba, the land of my ancestors, I was met with a grand reception from my boisterous and proud family. Amidst the attention and commotion, I felt both a sense of pride and discomfort, as if I had been thrust into a spotlight that I did not seek. As I reunited with my mother who had travelled there for a visit shortly before me and extended family, the warmth of their embrace brought comfort to my soul. The aroma of a welcome meal filled the air, inviting me to savour the flavours of home once again. Yet, amidst this joyous reunion, I carried with me the weight of responsibility — to understand the legacy of lateral violence that taints our community, even as we strive for unity and healing.

In the heart of South Sudan, where the echoes of history resound, I vowed to be a catalyst for change. To confront lateral violence and its intergenerational impact, we must tread carefully, unravelling its threads with compassion and empathy. Just as I listened to my brother's fears and concerns, we must listen to the silent cries of our people, to their wounds and struggles. The journey towards healing is not without challenges, but with determination and solidarity, we can rise above the scars of the past. Like the morning sun that pierces through the darkness, we shall banish the shadows of lateral violence, embracing unity and forgiveness. As we tread this path, let us embrace the paradox that in vulnerability lies strength, and in acknowledging our shared pain, we can forge a future where community violence is but a distant memory.

And just as my journey led me from the familiar shores of Melbourne to the embrace of my ancestral land, so too shall our collective journey lead us towards a nation and a community where community violence is but a chapter in the annals of history — a testament to the triumph of resilience and the power of unity.

In the midst of a family gathering, while we shared a meal,

a commotion erupted outside on the bustling streets of Juba. As we rushed to witness the scene, we encountered two young men entangled in a dispute over a motorbike fare. In a city where motorbikes darted through traffic like agile dancers, this altercation was a stark reminder of the dangers and tensions that permeated daily life. Lateral violence, like a poison seeping into the veins of a community, had permeated every aspect of society. It manifested in violent clashes between rival groups, spilling blood on the very streets that once witnessed the birth of a new nation. These divisions were not merely a result of external oppression alone, but rather a self-inflicted wound, as we turned against our own brethren instead of uniting against a common oppressor.

Within the customs and traditions of South Sudan, I witnessed the bench courts in action, where the ancient meets the modern in a delicate dance of justice. Amongst these courts, I encountered a case that etched itself into my memory forever. A young orphan, her life marred by violence, poverty and loss, stood bravely before the chiefs to reclaim her rightful inheritance—a small shop left behind by her deceased mother. However, her story unravelled a tale of unimaginable horror—a night that changed her life forever when her mother was killed, and she was brutally violated by her own uncle.

In the aftermath of war, survivors are often expected to return to normalcy, but the scars of conflict run deep, and the soul becomes a battlefield of its own. Even the strongest bridges have limits, and the weight of trauma can take its toll on even the bravest hearts. Soldiers who once protected the nation sometimes become the unwitting destroyers of their own communities, torn between duty and humanity. The impact of war lingers long after the battles have ceased, leaving a trail of emotional turmoil and vulnerability in the nation as well as abroad. Stereotypes fail to capture the complexity of the emotional processes at play, leading to misunderstandings and a failure to support those in need. To heal the wounds of community violence, we must delve deeper into the emotional stressors that perpetuate it, finding compassionate and effective interventions to break the cycle of violence.

As we reflect on the troubled past, we must also look forward to a future of healing and reconciliation. Just as a wounded phoenix rises from the ashes, so too can South Sudanese emerge from the depths of their traumas. It will be a journey of resilience and unity, where the hands that once wielded weapons now reach out to mend the broken pieces of the nation and its people souls. Together, we shall rewrite the narrative of South Sudanese, replacing the legacy of violence with one of healed people. Like a tapestry woven with threads of hope, we shall mend the torn fabric of our communities, uniting in the face of adversity. In the light of a new dawn, we shall honour the courage of the young girl who faced her tormentors with unwavering strength, heralding a future where justice and healing prevail.

With every step towards reconciliation, we shall bury the ghosts of community violence, bidding farewell to the shadow it cast upon our land. As the sun sets on the horizon, we shall forge a new destiny for South Sudan, where the resilience of its people shines like a guiding star, leading us towards a future of peace, unity, and boundless possibilities.

CHAPTER 7

MIGRATION TRAUMA

**From *The Rebel's Silhouette*
Faiz Ahmed Faiz, 1911 - 1984**

*When we launched life
on the river of grief,
how vital were our arms, how ruby our blood.
With a few strokes, it seemed,
we would cross all pain,
we would soon disembark.
That didn't happen.
In the stillness of each wave, we found invisible currents.
The boatmen, too, were unskilled,
their oars untested.
Investigate the matter as you will,
blame whomever, as much as you want,*

but the river hasn't changed,
the raft is still the same.
Now you suggest what's to be done,
you tell us how to come ashore.
When we saw the wounds of our country
appear on our skins,
we believed each word of the healers.
Besides, we remembered so many cures,
it seemed at any moment
all troubles would end, each wound heal completely.
That didn't happen: our ailments
were so many, so deep within us
that all diagnoses proved false, each remedy useless.
Now do whatever, follow each clue,
accuse whomever, as much as you will,
our bodies are still the same,
our wounds still open.
Now tell us what we should do,
you tell us how to heal these wounds.

In the crucible of survival mode that South Sudanese refugees
have endured for several years, the pain, suffering, and unattended wounds of trauma were frozen and stored within the
very fibres of their bodies, like ancient relics awaiting the dawn
of safety and security to permit their release and healing. In
those moments of desperation, every degree of their being was
devoted to meeting the relentless demands of survival, their

spirits resilient against the storm of adversity. The promise of reaching the shores of safety and peace became a beacon of hope, a sanctuary where the mending of shattered lives was said to commence.

However, even after finding refuge in foreign lands, the trauma information remained enmeshed in the core of their being, an indelible mark etched upon their personal field, as if to remind them of the scars that bear witness to their past. The location of this core being held the memories of those agonising moments, haunting them like relentless shadows that refused to fade. As refugees scattered across the world, fleeing persecution and violence, they carried the weight of their histories, each step marked by the echoes of their collective pain, as they sought solace and healing in the embrace of foreign lands.

The harrowing reality of survival mode leaves an indelible mark on the lives of refugees, with those from South Sudan bearing the weight of a particularly traumatic history. According to the United Nations High Commissioner for Refugees (UNHCR), South Sudan faces one of the most severe displacement crises globally, with millions of its citizens fleeing persecution and violence (UNHCR, 2023). Within the depths of their souls, the pain, suffering, and unattended wounds of trauma lay dormant, like deep tree roots, firmly embedded within the very fibres of their beings. The statistics provide a stark overview of the challenges South Sudanese refugees encounter. As of 2021, over 2.2 million people from South Sudan have sought refuge in neighbouring countries, with

Uganda hosting the largest number of refugees (UNHCR, 2023). In the crucible of desperation, every fibre of their being turns into a vessel of resilience, navigating through the treacherous waters of survival. The journey to safety is fraught with peril, as many refugees confront life-threatening dangers, including armed conflicts, hunger, and disease (UNHCR, 2023). Despite the overwhelming odds, they cling to hope with the tenacity of a lone flower breaking through the cracks of a desolate landscape, seeking the sun's warmth.

The promise of sanctuary serves as a guiding beacon, leading their weary souls towards the shores of safety and peace. For those who find refuge in foreign lands, the healing process becomes a delicate balance between confronting the traumas of the past—including the triggering experiences of settlement, racism, lack of resources, discrimination, and foreign laws—and embracing the possibilities of the future. The journey of a refugee transcends the mere physical escape from danger; it is a profound exploration of the self and a courageous quest to rediscover their place in a world that feels both familiar and foreign. As fellow humans, we must extend our hearts and hands to those who have endured unspeakable hardships. Within their stories lie the keys to understanding the true cost of violence and the remarkable resilience of the human spirit (UNHCR, 2023).

Once the waves of uncertainty carried them to the sanctuary of foreign lands, the weary travellers yearned to embrace the balm of healing. Yet, the trauma information, like a spectral spectre, refused to relinquish its hold, clinging to the core of their existence—an indelible mark etched upon their personal field, where memories of anguish and suffering lay enshrined.

As refugees dispersed across the world, they carried the weight of their histories like Atlas carrying the burden of the heavens upon his shoulders. Amidst foreign landscapes, they sought solace, yearning to heal the wounds inflicted upon their souls. Yet, like the phoenix rising from its ashes, the ghosts of their past cast long shadows upon their present.

Amidst the deviations of their journey, tempestuous winds of questions swirled: How does one find solace in a foreign land, far from the embrace of familiarity? Can the echoes of war be silenced, or do they reverberate in the recesses of the heart? Is it possible to mend the shattered pieces of a life once torn asunder by conflict? In their search for healing, the refugees were not mere wanderers but pilgrims on a quest for the elusive elixir of peace. Their wounds ran deep, their past scars tender to the touch, bearing the seeds of hope within the furrows of their collective spirit.

In this odyssey of suffering and resilience, they were not alone. The human family, a vast mosaic, shared in their triumphs and tribulations. The plight of the South Sudanese refugees, echoing across borders, became a universal call for compassion and empathy. The tapestry of humanity, woven with threads of diverse cultures, found unity in shared experiences of healing and growth. Amidst the shadows of despair, the indomitable human spirit emerged as a beacon of light. The refugees, like phoenixes rising from adversity, embodied strength born from vulnerability. Their journey towards healing, fraught with challenges, held the promise of renewal in the seeds of hope nestled within their hearts.

As of 2023, the global spread of South Sudanese refugees, numbering 2.4 million, with over 2.2 million seeking refuge in neighbouring countries and beyond (UNHCR, 2023), signifies the largest refugee crisis in Africa. This diaspora of individuals, families, and communities attests to the far-reaching impact of violence and conflict in their homeland. The exodus from South Sudan has woven a web of displacement, with refugees scattering across regions in search of safety and solace.

In neighbouring countries like Uganda, Sudan, Ethiopia, and Kenya, a significant number of South Sudanese refugees have found refuge, each carrying the weight of personal stories and collective trauma. The borders they crossed, often on foot and under perilous conditions, delineate despair from hope, a past marked by violence from a future yearning for peace. Beyond the immediate region, South Sudanese refugees have forged new lives on other continents, including the United States, Canada, Australia, and various European nations, marked by resilience as they adapt to foreign cultures and societies, all while carrying memories of their homeland and dreams of a brighter tomorrow.

The global spread of South Sudanese refugees highlights the urgent need to address the root causes of the multilayered violence and conflict in their homeland. It serves as a poignant reminder of the interconnectedness of human suffering and the collective responsibility of the international community to provide protection and support to those displaced by wars and persecution. Amidst such displacement and upheaval, the stories of South Sudanese refugees stand as powerful testaments to the resilience of the human spirit and the enduring hope for a world free of violence. As witnesses to their journeys, we are called to stand in solidarity, extending empathy, actionable solutions, and working collectively towards a future where peace, justice, and reconciliation prevail—not only for the South Sudanese but for all humanity enduring immense suffering.

In life's grand tapestry, threads of sorrow and joy, suffering and healing are intricately woven together. As refugees continue their journey, they carry the collective hope for a brighter future, where past wounds are tended with compassion and love. Becoming ambassadors of peace in foreign lands, they bridge humanity's divides with empathy's golden thread.

Thus, the journey of South Sudanese refugees transcends a mere chapter in their history; it becomes a testament to the human spirit's resilience. Their stories, like timeless poems etched into time's annals, inspire us to confront violence's shadows and embrace healing's light. In their peace pursuit, they remind us that every heart holds transformation potential, and every journey harbours renewal possibility. Let us heed their call, joining hands to forge a world where human rights and dignities are respected, and healing is paramount.

Amidst the darkness that envelops them, a flicker of hope emerges, like a lone star piercing through the night sky. In the face of such adversity, the human spirit reveals its remarkable resilience, akin to a phoenix rising from the ashes of despair.

Each refugee becomes a living testament to the strength of the human will to survive and the unwavering determination to rebuild amidst the ruins of their lives. They are not merely victims of circumstance, but warriors of courage, perseverance, and hope.

Within the refugee's heart, a delicate dance unfolds between hope and despair. Like a pendulum swaying between two worlds, they grapple with the weight of their past and the uncertain terrain of their future. The journey of refuge is not a linear path; it weaves through a labyrinth of emotions, a maze of conflicting feelings. Deep within, they carry the echoes of their homeland, a distant melody that haunts their dreams. They yearn for a place to call home, a sanctuary where their weary souls can find solace. Yet, in their search for refuge, they confront the invisible scars of trauma—wounds not visible to the naked eye but etched upon the very fabric of their existence. These scars affect how they perceive the world, shaping their interactions and colouring their experiences.

As they navigate the uncharted waters of displacement, they seek a path to reclaim their lost sense of self, like a ship lost at sea yearning for a guiding star. In this journey of suffering and survival, refugees transform into poets of resilience, painters of hope, and composers of courage. Their stories transcend tales of pain and suffering, evolving into narratives of triumph over adversity, where the human spirit soars against all odds.

Their journey illustrates the complexity of the human experience, a place where darkness and light converge in a dance of paradox. Moving forward, they grapple with a riddle of identity, striving to reconcile the fragments of their shattered lives into a new tapestry of meaning. Like alchemists of the soul, they transform the lead of their traumas into the gold of healing and growth. The refugee journey becomes a collective ode to the indomitable human spirit, a symphony of survival composed amidst chaos.

As we bear witness to their odyssey, we are reminded of humanity's fragility and resilience. Their journey becomes a mirror to our own, as we all navigate the currents of joy and sorrow, hope and despair. Their stories invite us to stand in solidarity, to extend compassion, and to recognise our shared humanity. In their quest for sanctuary, refugees become ambassadors of empathy, teaching us about human connection and the significance of a welcoming embrace. Their journey challenges us to dismantle the walls we build, both physical and emotional, urging us to reconsider the meaning of home. For ultimately, the essence of refuge is found not in a place but in the hearts of those who open their arms to welcome the displaced.

As the sun sets on their journey, the refugees emerge as torchbearers of hope, illuminating the path towards a world where compassion triumphs over indifference, where understanding conquers fear, and where the human family stands united in solidarity. In their quest for refuge, they remind us that the resilience of the human spirit knows no bounds, and that amidst the darkest nights, a beacon of hope will always shine. Let us heed their call and create a world where every heart finds a home, and every soul is embraced with compassion and actionable solutions.

In the embrace of the unknown, refugees navigate a new reality where their identities, once anchored to their homeland, are now interwoven with the intricate tapestry of their refugee status. The challenges they encounter extend beyond the external to the deeply internal, necessitating a soul-searching voyage to rediscover their place in a world that feels both familiar and foreign. Amidst the chaos of displacement, empathy and understanding shine as guiding lights. As fellow humans, it is our duty to extend our hearts and hands to those who have endured unspeakable hardships. Within their stories lie the keys to grasping the true cost of violence and the resilience of the human spirit.

As we delve into the reality of refugee violence and trauma, we enter a realm where the wounds of the past meld with the uncertainty of the present. This landscape is scarred by displacement, loss, and the relentless quest for survival—a reality that calls for more than mere physical healing. Indeed, the journey towards healing transcends the repair of physical wounds; it ventures into the realms of emotional, psychological, mental, and spiritual rejuvenation.

As we accompany those who have sought refuge from the horrors of violence, we must be guided not only by their present acts but by what happened to them. The wounds they carry are not mere surface scratches but profound lacerations that have pierced their souls. To heal these deep wounds, we must be willing to walk beside them on their journey, offering our support and understanding. Healing is not an instant remedy; it is a process that requires time, preparation for repair, care, and empathy. The scars of trauma cannot be erased overnight or punished away by imprisonment, nor can the pain be numbed with quick fixes. Instead, we must steadfastly commit to being present, to listening, and to validating the emotions of those who have endured unimaginable hardships. Therefore, in this collective journey, we should strive to build a future where violence finds no place, and peace becomes the guiding light. The stories of resilience and survival carried by refugees become beacons of hope amidst the darkness. As we hold their hands, we offer them a glimpse of hope—a promise that healing is possible, and they are not alone in their struggle. In the narratives of refugees, we discover the power to shape a world that embraces compassion and understanding. Their stories serve as powerful reminders of the strength of the human spirit—the indomitable will to endure, heal, and thrive against all odds. Together, we forge a path towards a future where trauma is transformed into strength. It is a journey that requires the collective effort of communities, institutions, and nations. The scars of violence and displacement are not isolated experiences but collective wounds that call for collective intervention and prevention.

As we embrace the stories of refugees and acknowledge the pain they carry, we sow the seeds of compassion that bloom into lasting healing. Through our solidarity and support, we create an environment where trauma finds solace in understanding, resilience finds nourishment in community, and hope shines as a guiding star.

Let us stand together, hand in hand, as we walk alongside

those seeking refuge and healing. For in their journey, we find the strength to build a world that transcends violence—a world that embraces the transformative power of compassion and fosters the lasting healing of the human spirit. As we embark on this journey together, we become witnesses to the resilience of the human heart—a resilience capable of rebuilding shattered lives and forging a future where violence is replaced with peace.

CHAPTER 8

THE PAST IN
THE PRESENT

"The Americans gave it a name, PTSD — Post Traumatic Stress Disorder. I had heard about it before: it was something that had to do with army men coming back from the frontline, veterans who had been under a lot of stress. Or survivors of terrorist attacks, bombings, massacres, or big accidents. No worries though. I was doing just fine, as I'd tell myself. At the end of the day, I genuinely believed it: I never really took as many risks as many of the colleagues I had met or shared the most traumatic experiences in the

*field with, hence I had probably been exposed to
a lot less stress".*

*- Marco Lupis, Il male inutile: Dal Kosovo a
Timor Est, dal Chiapas a Bali, le testimoni-
anze di un reporter di guerra*

Marco Lupis explained a very relatable experiences of
exposer and experiences of trauma for many South Sudanese
people who were not technically war veterans but had experienced secondary trauma.

Historical Trauma

The concept of historical trauma serves as a profound illustra-
tion of how suffering is interconnected and its lasting impact
across generations. Picture a river flowing steadily through
time, carrying the collective pain, anguish, and struggles of
people bound by a common identity, affiliation, or circumstance. This river, fed by the tears of those torn from their
homes, the desecration of their sacred sites, the silencing of
their language, and the brutalization of their essence, carves
a deep wound into the psyche of the affected community.
Historical trauma is a force that intertwines through the fabric
of culture and society, leaving scars that resonate through the
ages.

When we examine history's tapestry, we encounter the devastating outcomes of wars, imperial ambitions, colonization, and

domination. Each instance of this collective suffering paints a grim portrait of cultural, political, racial, ethnic, religious, gender, and sexual extermination, driven by systemic intolerance. As the river of historical trauma flows, it merges the narratives of those who have weathered its painful waves, creating a potent current that reaches across generations.

At public panels and conferences, these historical tragedies are dissected, often by academics or advocates. Among those discussing South Sudan's past, a poignant question arises, drawing a parallel with another chapter of heartbreak in history—the Holocaust. They inquire, with a sense of perplexity, whether South Sudanese can heal as some Holocaust survivors have. This inquiry underscores the complexities of trauma and the distinctive ways it manifests across different communities.

Comparing the pain and experiences of diverse communities is a simplistic approach that overlooks the multifaceted nature of suffering and healing. It's not meaningful to juxtapose the trauma experiences to determine who has suffered the most or who is healing quicker than others. For example, comparing the conflicts between Israel and Hamas-led Palestinians, the war in Russia and Ukraine, the situation in Afghanistan, or the unrest in Myanmar—and questioning which victims and survivors should or will recover from these traumas faster—is not constructive. These conflicts share a common thread: civilian suffering. Thousands, including the elderly and children, have been killed, witnessing death and displacement (Ben-Ezra et al., 2023). The emphasis in these nations and among these people should be on ensuring safety and fostering healing, rather than speculating on when and who will heal and move on from the past, especially when, for many, the pain persists despite the passage of years.

Comparing experiences of pain and healing misses the point, as each experience of violence and war leaves nothing but long-term, generational, and intergenerational suffering that requires a collective effort to address and heal.

Time, as a relentless witness to historical events, weaves its threads into the fabric of a community's memory. The living memory of traumatic events can be both a burden and a source of resilience, anchoring communities to their past while propelling their pursuit of justice and healing. The ongoing struggles for peace and reconciliation add further layers of complexity, as communities grapple with the lingering impacts of violence and seek paths to coexistence.

In exploring historical trauma, we encounter the profound truth that scars run deep not only in the persecuted but also in the persecutors. A shared history of suffering binds both victims and perpetrators, creating a tangled web of collective pain. The human psyche, intimately connected to culture and community, perceives any threat to the integrity of one's culture as a threat to their very core. Thus, the trauma of loss and persecution reverberates far beyond the initial event, echoing through generations and shaping the identities and behaviours of individuals and communities alike. The impact of historical trauma extends far beyond a mere event of the past; it becomes a living presence that shapes the present and future. The echoes of past injustices continue to reverberate through generations, influencing how individuals perceive the world, relate to one another, and respond to challenges. This trauma becomes ingrained within the collective consciousness, influencing cultural practices, norms, and traditions.

Understanding historical trauma requires us to resist the temptation to compare suffering, for such comparisons negate the unique and deeply personal experiences of each community. Instead, we must embrace the richness of diversity in human experiences and the multifaceted ways trauma unfolds within different cultural contexts. To address historical trauma and foster healing, we must acknowledge the importance of cultural identity and the interwoven nature of individual and communal well-being. Recognizing the complexity of trauma enables us to cultivate compassion and repair, creating spaces where diverse voices can be heard and acknowledged.

As we navigate the intricate layers of suffering and healing, we must approach historical trauma with humility and an open heart. Each community's journey represents a narrative of resilience, survival, and transformation—a testament to the enduring power of the human spirit. By honouring the uniqueness of these stories and fostering a spirit of understanding, we lay the foundation for a future where collective healing is achievable, and where the echoes of historical trauma may find solace in the embrace of shared humanity.

Navigating the complexities of historical trauma necessitates an embrace of the immense task of healing and reconciliation. The wounds may run deep, but through compassion, understanding, and a dedication to fostering a culture of healing, we can begin to mend the torn fabric of our collective humanity. By recognising the scars of the past and striving towards a future of unity and acceptance, we pave the way for a brighter, more resilient tomorrow for all those who have endured the ravages of historical trauma.

Intergenerational Trauma

In the vast and complex web of human existence, the internal conflicts we face and the societal challenges we confront are reflections of larger wars experienced and witnessed back in South Sudan. The young nation, marred by instability and civil unrest even after gaining independence, faces numerous hurdles in its quest to build a cohesive society and functional state. This journey towards nation-building is fraught with reports of violence, lawlessness, and injustice, impacting both systemic and individual levels. The scars of war and trauma, etched into the collective psyche, echo far beyond South Sudan's borders.

The violence that has come to define South Sudan's struggles extends beyond its geographical confines, manifesting in the diaspora. Among South Sudanese communities in countries like Australia, a concerning trend has emerged, particularly among younger generations and their families, entangling them in the criminal justice system and media spotlight due to a range of crimes, from murders and assaults to armed robberies, sexual assaults, and domestic violence. The transition in the diaspora is marked by challenges, with the disintegration of family units propelled by various factors, leading to an increase in single mothers and female-led households.

In the realm where single mothers are left to raise their children alone in foreign lands—where it no longer "takes a village to raise a child"—a complex interplay of challenges unfolds. These courageous women face not only the difficulties of adapting to a new environment but also their own traumas, often navigating the Western lifestyle's maze and its unrestrained freedoms. Many bear the scars of absent fathers and personal violations, seeking validation and love in fleeting relationships. Unbeknownst to them, this quest for fulfilment often overlooks their children's need for connection and co-regulation, leaving them in a state of perpetual uncertainty and anxiety.

Furthermore, countries with lower rates of single-parent-led households often enjoy higher economic advantages, contrasting regions like South Sudan and its diaspora. The incidence of relative poverty among single-parent families is notably lower in Sweden compared to the United States, Canada, and Australia. This highlights that while family structure may influence societal violence rates, the broader social and economic frameworks, coupled with psychological challenges, play a more significant role in determining violence levels.

The unintentional neglect stems from the circumstances imposed upon them, raising multiple children alone in a foreign Western country where financial independence is paramount. Often lacking advanced education and employed in low-skilled, casual jobs, these mothers depend on their children to navigate the complexities of the Australian systems. This role reversal disempowers the parents and alters family dynamics, with older children taking on parental roles, effectively parenting their parents and altering the household's power balance. Consequently, the emotional needs of these young individuals remain unmet as they grapple with emotions that have been either frightening, confusing, or absent in their caregivers. Instead of fostering healthy growth through meaningful connections, they experience incoherence, numbness, or anxiety.

Many young individuals grow up without the presence of fathers or positive male role models during critical development stages (Anyieth, 2021). The absence of fathers manifests in various ways, each impacting the child's emotional well-being (Farrell & Gray, 2019). Some fathers are involuntarily absent, as the mother restricts their access to the children due to a violent history. Others may be physically present but emotionally unavailable, struggling with their psychological issues, rendering them incapable of forming meaningful connections with their children (Farrell & Gray, 2019). The effects of absent fathers are profound, leading to a crisis of identity and self-worth among affected children. They question their place in the world, pondering why their fathers are either absent or only recognize their existence upon achieving something significant (Anyieth, 2021).

For children and young individuals who receive praise solely based on performance, validation becomes conditional and harmful. They adopt the belief that their worth depends on continuous success, pushing themselves excessively for attention and validation. This mindset can leave them feeling inadequate if they fail to excel in traditional academic subjects like mathematics, science, or English, as they internalize the belief that they cannot match up to their high-performing peers (Farrell & Gray, 2019).

The void in these children's lives propels them to seek acceptance, validation, and self-worth outside their family units, leading to the formation of cliques and groups. Initially, these groups emerge as a quest for belonging and acceptance but can tragically escalate into violent confrontations. Observations suggest that the streets become mentors and monitors for these vulnerable souls, guiding them on a path fraught with danger and trauma. Tragically, there have been instances where young South Sudanese individuals have lost their lives to fellow community members or, in acts of desperation, have taken their own lives through suicide. These grim incidents, often labelled as gang-driven, arise from a complex web of factors, including upbringing, generational and intergenerational trauma, and environmental stressors. While genetics and nurture contribute, it is crucial to recognize that many of these youths are not inherently criminals.

What their parents often fail to realize, as they navigate parenthood burdened by their traumas, is that without proper monitoring and mentorship, especially for boys, the streets will fill the void, potentially exacerbating the traumas passed down from one generation to the next. A child's first experience of love and acceptance should come from their parents or primary caregivers (Farrell & Gray, 2019). If these caregivers' nervous systems are hyperactive or shut down due to unresolved traumas, they become an unstable anchor for the child (Farrell & Gray, 2019). Consequently, the child may feel adrift, like an astronaut in their own body, lacking adequate orientation and stability. As they mature, they become isolated within themselves, disconnected from their emotions, and a reflection of their traumatized inheritance, oscillating between hyperarousal and dysregulation or freezing and numbing. Parents, carers, and practitioners may notice violent behaviours but often overlook the deeper void these young individuals are attempting to fill with their actions.

As South Sudanese families in the diaspora confront these challenges, the enduring effects of violence and trauma continue to influence their experiences. Healing the wounds of war and addressing intergenerational trauma demand tackling these complex issues and offering support and understanding to those rebuilding their lives in foreign lands. The path to reconciliation and resilience involves not only the South Sudanese communities but the broader human family, extending compassion and resources to help them reclaim their sense of self-worth and find solace in shared humanity.

The healing and transformation journey for these individuals necessitates a collective effort from the community, society, and beyond. It requires compassionate understanding of the traumas they bear, a commitment to providing support, and a resolve to mend the fractured pieces of their lives. By fostering a nurturing and empathetic environment that empowers them, we can guide these young individuals toward reconciliation, self-discovery, and actualization. Healing the wounds of the past and building a future where violence and trauma give way to love, acceptance, and growth can only be achieved through our collective support and action.

In the tumultuous journey of self-discovery, young South Sudanese individuals find themselves navigating the delicate balance between a yearning for acceptance and the weight of unresolved traumas. Feeling unheard and misunderstood, they sculpt their identities from their interpretations of acceptance in a seemingly indifferent world. Regrettably, these self-crafted identities often lead them down hazardous paths, causing harm to themselves and others. Alienated from their families and seeking companionship among peers with similar experiences, they forge bonds based on misguided perceptions of masculinity—associating toughness, delinquency, and violence with being a "real man." This warped view of masculinity serves as a defence against past emotional wounds, providing temporary validation and a sense of empowerment. In their quest for strength and autonomy, they overlook the profound impact of their actions, perpetuating a cycle of violence that ensnares many South Sudanese youth, both in their homeland and abroad.

As I contemplate the plight of two generations of South Sudanese, born and raised amid war, adversity, and its lingering effects, a profound sense of desolation overwhelms me. The magnitude of trauma they've endured appears daunting, leaving one to wonder about the starting point for healing our community from this scourge. Yet, despite the despair, succumbing to hopelessness is not an option. Our initial step involves grasping the intricacies of trauma and violence, exploring its roots before embarking on intervention and prevention.

In the swiftly evolving landscape of acculturation, young people assimilate into Western societies at an alarming rate, influenced by a pop culture that often glamorizes violence and dysfunction. The portrayal of life in media, films, and on social platforms does not entirely mirror the realities and values of Western society. This cultural clash, particularly between younger generations eager to embrace new ways and older ones aiming to preserve traditional values, results in community dissonance. As these cultural currents move at differing paces, communication fragments, intensifying the struggle to adapt amidst the burdens of both old and new traumas.

The starkness of cultural transitions and unaddressed traumas obscures clear understanding and connection across generations and communities. Efforts to bridge the gap between South Sudanese culture, mainstream Western culture, and Black American culture resemble a comedy of errors—endeavours to reconcile diverse identities in a world where trauma remains unhealed and connections fractured.

Amidst this turmoil lies a call to make sense of both past and present experiences. To navigate the maze of trauma and violence, we must foster open dialogue, empathy, and a dedication to healing our community's deep-seated wounds. Only through united efforts and a collective resolve can we reconcile these disparate forces and chart a course toward a future where violence and trauma no longer dominate our narrative.

In the vast expanse of the South Sudanese diaspora, the generational gap intertwines with the stark realities of racism and discrimination, culminating in a heart-wrenching epidemic of suicides among young people in our community across Australia. Almost every other month, news of another young life lost to suicide or at the hands of fellow South Sudanese shakes us to the core. The intergenerational trauma they endure, coupled with disconnection from their parents and the struggle for identity, culture, and a place in the West, creates a suffocating sense of hopelessness. For these young souls, life loses its meaning, and their voices seem muted in both school and home environments. They yearn for understanding and acceptance but find themselves bullied at school and disconnected from their parents, who struggle to comprehend their experiences.

In this struggle for survival, it becomes evident that the death of the soul, the self, or the psyche is far more significant than the death of the physical body. The sacrifice of the body becomes a desperate measure to preserve the self, the mind, and the sense of identity. A stable, integrated sense of selfhood develops through the nurturing relationships and cultural experiences one encounters within the community. The psyche relies on the nourishment of cultural values and connections as much as the body relies on sustenance from food. The link between culture and character is an inseparable socio-psychological reality. A perceived threat to one's culture is seen as a threat to one's very being and ethical value system, intricately binding the individual to their culture and vice versa. The loss of culture is akin to the loss of self, and the prioritisation of honour, self-respect, and the preservation of one's group and culture become paramount. This human propensity to protect honour and identity, even at the expense of physical comfort and survival, sets us apart from other species.

The complex emotional forces of shame, pride, guilt, and innocence come into play, driving individuals and groups to act violently towards others or themselves in the face of perceived humiliation or loss of face. The loss of self-esteem is akin to the death of the self, and this fear of disintegration drives people to great lengths to protect their individual or group identity.

In this whirlwind of emotions and cultural clashes, we must confront the intersections that make a human being's life worth living. To address the alarming rates of suicide and violence in our community, we must first understand and address the underlying traumas and sense of loss that young people face. Only then can we begin the journey of healing and transformation, bridging the gap between generations and fostering a sense of belonging and hope for the future. It is through this collective effort that we can hope to break the cycle of violence and trauma, forging a path towards a brighter and more unified community.

Intergenerational trauma is a profound force that weaves its threads through the tapestry of family, community, and society, leaving an indelible mark on the human experience. Its effects are not confined to a single moment in time; instead, they reverberate along a vertical line, stretching back through the ages, connecting past, present, and future. Like a haunting melody that echoes through generations, the legacy of untreated and severe trauma passes from one family member to the next, leaving a lasting imprint on the collective psyche.

Epigenetic factors play a significant role in perpetuating the intergenerational transmission of trauma. These factors carry the imprints of past suffering in the very essence of those yet to be born, creating a biological memory that extends beyond individual lifetimes. The experiences of our ancestors become etched into our DNA, shaping not only our physical characteristics but also influencing our emotional responses and mental health.

Imagine a family tree, its branches reaching back through time, each bearing the weight of its unique traumas and hardships. As we trace the lineage of these experiences, we begin to understand how the scars of the past have shaped the present and continue to influence the future. The pain of one generation is passed down to the next, and the burden of unresolved trauma is carried forward, often manifesting in patterns of behaviour and coping mechanisms.

Intergenerational trauma is not merely a recounting of historical events; it is a living, breathing force that permeates family dynamics and social structures. Unhealed wounds from the past can manifest in unhealthy relationships, substance abuse, violence, and other destructive behaviours that reverberate through generations. The impact of intergenerational trauma is far-reaching, extending beyond individual families to entire communities and societies. Communities scarred by historical injustices and violence often experience a collective sense of pain and loss, affecting social cohesion and trust. The trauma becomes ingrained within the cultural fabric, shaping belief systems, norms, and even the ways societies respond to external challenges.

Breaking the cycle of intergenerational trauma requires a profound commitment to improving all areas of human life. Acknowledging the deep-rooted wounds of the past is a critical step in dismantling the legacy of suffering and creating a pathway towards transformation and healing. By fostering open dialogue, empathy, understanding, and providing resources, we can create spaces for collective healing and reconciliation. Interventions aimed at addressing intergenerational trauma must consider not only individual healing but also the healing of family systems and communities. Offering support, resources, and trauma- and culturally sensitive interventions can help individuals and communities begin the journey towards healing the wounds of the past and building a future free from the chains of inherited trauma.

Imagine a torch passed from hand to hand, each bearer carrying not only the warmth of the flame but also the burden of unresolved pain and suffering. Families become torchbearers of intergenerational trauma, transmitting its effects through generations. The bonds within the family, the very fabric of their identity, become interwoven with implicit messages encoded by past traumas, leaving imprints often unexamined and unresolved.

The consequences of intergenerational trauma manifest in myriad ways. Children born into this legacy find themselves navigating a landscape fraught with poverty, abuse, and susceptibility to mental and physical illness. Their lives, shaped by the unseen hands of trauma, become challenging to carve paths of meaning and purpose. In some heart-wrenching instances, mothers who themselves suffered the scars of generational childhood sexual abuse find, to their shock, that their children have endured the same pain. They hoped to shield their offspring from harm, but instead, the cycle of abuse perpetuated itself, shrouding the family in dissociation, detachment, and silence. The echoes of past trauma play out in these intergenerational cycles of abuse, leading to the tragedy of children and young people suffering as their parents did before them.

The journey through trauma is seldom straightforward. Traumatised individuals may find themselves inexplicably drawn to situations that mirror their original trauma, as witnessed often within our community. Like a magnet tugging at their souls, they seem compelled to expose themselves to circumstances reminiscent of their past suffering. These behavioural re-enactments often elude conscious understanding, carrying the imprints of earlier life experiences awaiting reconciliation. Moreover, the consequences of trauma do not remain confined to individual experiences. As these patterns of unconscious re-enactment perpetuate, they extend beyond the individual and seep into the fabric of society, enacting a cycle of violence that reverberates through the collective consciousness.

In the hands of researchers like myself, the stories of trauma victims are brought to light, uncovering a startling pattern. The traumas they have endured, like spectres from the past, continue to manifest in the present. As if caught in a never-ending play, these individuals unconsciously re-en-act their prior victimisation, perpetuating a cycle that seems unbreakable. Understanding the impact of intergenerational trauma, as well as other forms of traumatic experiences within the South Sudanese communities, is crucial in addressing the societal violence that follows. By acknowledging the echoes of past suffering and striving to break the cycle of trauma, we can embark on the challenging journey towards healing and reconciliation. Just as a skilled conductor leads an orchestra, guiding the musicians to blend their individual melodies into a unified symphony, we must discover ways to harmonise the discord of intergenerational trauma into a collective journey towards healing. Only then can we hope to liberate ourselves from the chains of the past and forge a future where the legacy of trauma is transformed into a legacy of resilience and hope.

CHAPTER 9

STRUCTURAL VIOLENCE TRAUMA

In the echoes of time, "The Prophet," Khalil Gibran, stood as a harbinger of wisdom, shedding light on society's relentless condemnation and lack of compassion for its criminals and sinners. He beckoned us not to reduce the offender to a mere animal, a creature to be subjugated and ostracized, but instead, implored us to delve deep into the recesses of their disadvantaged position in society. To understand the roots of their delinquency, to seek empathy amidst the abyss of judgment – this, the Prophet proclaimed, was the true reflection of a compassionate and responsible society.

Upon arriving in Australia, we harboured the hopeful notion of a land where "we are young and free," as the national anthem resounds. However, we quickly realized that this declaration did not seem to extend to black people – the indigenous, black migrants, and refugees like ourselves. Our black youth, though young, were far from free.

In this land, black youth bore the weight of their skin colour, standing tall but burdened by a profound legacy of trauma – generational, environmental, racism, bullying, and discrimination – leaving deep scars on their souls. This trauma, inflicted not only by peers but sometimes even by educators, laid their plight bare before us, profoundly impacting their lives. With barriers to employment, literacy and language issues, and economic hardships, they became easy targets for violence.

In the book *"Boy Do You Wanna Give Me Some Action"* by Bec Smith, a project birthed from Flemington and Kensington Community Legal Centre, now known as West Justice, we glimpsed the disturbing reality of police targeting young African boys, seemingly out of sheer boredom, to fulfil their arrest quotas, regardless of these youths' innocence. Prejudice was evident even before officers exited their vehicles, their hands already reaching for instruments of pain. The boys were stripped of their humanity, belittled, and devalued on the streets, in schools, and within the very fabric of this country they called home. In educational institutions, many were relegated to the bottom, labelled as needing to "catch up," and denied an environment that allows young people to flourish.

These individuals are not mere campaign policies; they are sons, daughters, brothers, and sisters – young people with dreams and aspirations. It doesn't take a legal expert to see the injustice in this. Rehabilitation is often an afterthought, if considered at all, inadvertently fostering a cycle of criminality. When they attempted to express their pain, their voices were often diminished to their age and race, leaving them feeling frustrated and isolated. They longed to be heard, understood, and treated as equals.

"*Why are you so angry?*" they are asked when they resist this oppressive tide. Yet, if they had been truly listened to, if their grievances had been acknowledged and addressed, perhaps their anger could have been alleviated. Instead, they found themselves ensnared in a maelstrom of prejudice and hostility, pushed to the edge of desperation. Amidst these inequalities, they sought solace in their own ways, for the system had failed them, leaving them to navigate a world that seldom saw them as equals.

In the shadow of this landscape of injustice, the souls of our black youth yearn for systemic restructuring, resource redistribution, and compassion. As we delve into the heart of these inequalities and traumas, the call for understanding, cultural, and systemic actions becomes louder. Within these echoes of suffering lie the seeds of transformation and redemption.

Amidst the struggles of South Sudanese families, the haunting spectre of extreme poverty and discrimination looms large, casting a long shadow over their lives. In the echoes of their stories, we find a truth resonating with Gandhi's profound observation that the deadliest form of violence is poverty. Each passing day brings the realisation that understanding their violent behaviour solely through an individual lens is futile and misguided. To truly grasp the essence of violence, we must delve deeper into the heart of structural violence that plagues this nation. Amidst this land of opportunity and hope, we must resist the temptation to scapegoat those who appear different, those who have recently migrated in pursuit of a better life. Our focus must shift towards the structural causes of violent death, far more significant in numerical, public health, and human terms. Behold "structural violence," a malevolent force manifesting as increased rates of poverty, crime, death, and disability among those at society's lowest rungs. The stark contrast with those experiencing relatively lower death rates exposes the consequences of society's collective choices regarding wealth distribution.

These tragedies are not acts of God or natural ends of life expectancy, but rather outcomes of societal decisions and attitudes. It is crucial to differentiate "structural violence" from "behavioural violence." The former exerts its lethal influence continuously, insidiously infiltrating lives, while the latter occurs sporadically in individual acts of violence against one another. Structural violence operates independently of specific individuals and their actions, yet its effects are enduring and pervasive. Often cloaked in invisibility, this form of violence can mask itself behind other causes, rendering it challenging to discern its true nature. Only by adopting an epidemiological perspective of public health and preventive medicine can we reveal its existence, scope, and lethal impact. The landscape of evidence is clear; in Australia, Black people, whether indigenous, immigrants, or refugees, face higher mortality rates than their white Anglo-Saxon counterparts.

Attributing these deaths solely to individual behaviour would be a serious misjudgement. A deeper exploration into preventive medicine uncovers the underlying structural and economic factors perpetuating this tragic reality. The relative deprivation and poverty weighing more heavily on black communities than on their white counterparts contribute to this cycle of suffering and death. This intricate web is woven by unequal access to healthcare, racial discrimination, and social rejection – factors that exacerbate the trauma of pre- and post-migration experiences.

Trapped within this labyrinth of social and economic structures, South Sudanese communities grapple with the consequences of an unjust system. High blood pressure, common among urbanised African blacks in America, the West Indies, and South Africa, serves as a stark reminder of the profound impact of socioeconomic structures. When exposed to the class and caste hierarchies of the West, both whites and blacks witness an escalation in violence.

In this politically charged discourse, the true nature of violence remains obscured, often overlooked, and underappreciated. When violence is criminalised, it commands attention and concern. Yet, when it arises as a consequence of our social and economic structures, it fades into the background, becoming invisible. To truly comprehend this complex situation, we must confront the burden of proof, challenging those who fail to recognise the grave implications of our socioeconomic structure on the excess deaths of the most vulnerable among us.

At the heart of these inequalities, seen as traumas, the call for reform becomes clear, urging us to dismantle the oppressive forces that stifle hope and sow the seeds of violence. Only by confronting these structural terrors can we truly liberate ourselves from the shadows of violence and chart a path towards a more equitable and compassionate society.

Within the confines of this nation, the grim reality of structural violence and its deadly implications paints a disheartening picture. An uncomfortable truth unfolds before us—that we often seek to blame individuals rather than confront the roots of violence. Structural violence, intertwined with the fabric of society, lies at the heart of behavioural violence, forming an inseparable cause-and-effect relationship.

As we explore the sociological landscape, a pressing question arises—what circumstances push individuals to the brink of violent behaviour, overwhelmed by shame as discussed in previous chapters, and desperation? Identifying the groups subjected to disproportionate shame and discrimination presents a complex challenge, as it risks reducing them solely to their victimisation, overlooking the array of their triumphs and strengths. This discussion carries a bitter irony as we consider the plight of the South Sudanese community, often deemed prone to high levels of violent crime, while historical evidence shows that the violence inflicted upon black communities by whites far outweighs any violence they have committed in return.

Delving into the psychological dimensions of different social classes, we uncover the power of systematic shaming and humiliation as a catalyst for violence. Edith Jacobson's observations reveal that shame can be instilled through low financial, social, or racial status, highlighting the exposure to shaming experienced by certain population groups in our society. The poor, trapped in the "lower class" labels, bear the weight of society's indifference, yearning for recognition yet condemned to invisibility. This deprivation of fame denies them the chance to experience pride, leaving them vulnerable to shame.

In this analysis, we must acknowledge the complexities of visibility. While the spotlight on one's achievements nurtures pride, its focus on flaws inflicts shame. Fame augments pride, whereas infamy enhances shame. The poor seek recognition and admiration but face disdain and attack, stripped of the dignity they desire. This cycle of disdain, as Hannah Arendt highlighted, compounds the curse of poverty with the insult of oblivion, further injuring the lives of the oppressed.

For the black population in America, this struggle for visibility assumes a grimmer aspect. The legacy of slavery casts a shadow of obscurity, making the enslaved "wholly overlooked." Black authors have vividly depicted the experience of invisibility, detailing the profound shame imposed upon them. The cycle persists as black refugees become part of the most marginalised groups, starting from absolute nothingness.

Yet, in the shadows of shame and deprivation, the wealthy flourish, monopolising the nation's resources and power, undisturbed by the exploited black and white communities. The peace of the privileged is bought at the expense of the suffering of the oppressed, perpetuating a cycle of violence rooted in systemic injustice.

As we address the nexus of inequalities and traumas, a call to action resonates—to break the chains of structural violence, to illuminate the darkness of invisibility, and to pave the way for a fairer, more compassionate society. Only through collective responsibility and solidarity can we redefine the narrative of violence, creating a world where every individual is heard and dignified. In this shared endeavour, our humanity shines brightly, leading us to a future free from the grip of violence and despair.

Class and Caste

In the intricate needlepoint of society, a difficult revelation emerges—those who occupy lower statuses in class and caste are bound to the shadows of violence. How can we unravel the enigma of this connection? To illustrate, let's consider the work of Sennett and Cobb (2023) as an example. Their journey into the depths of the American social class, unfolding through poignant interviews with labourers and their families, sheds light on a contest for dignity that the disadvantaged seem destined to lose.

Within class distinctions, a morality of shaming and humiliation reigns, eroding the sense of self-worth and pride of those trapped in the lower echelons. The emotional impact is marked by impudent snobbery, a relentless putdown that leaves scars on the soul. The social conditions bear a weight of shame, plunging individuals into a bottomless abyss of inadequacy, with no respite from this unrelenting torment.

The ascription of weakness, forced upon the lower class, casts an enduring spell of vulnerability, as this weakness becomes intrinsic to their being. The post-Coronavirus pandemic era exacerbates our struggles, with the cost of living skyrocketing, leaving us grappling with immense suffering. The loss of vehicles and homes to repossession amplifies their sense of injured dignity, as those on the lowest rung of the ladder express resentment at being treated as less than human—no more than mere "woodwork" in the grand scheme of society.

From the depths of obscurity, a haunting question lingers, unspoken but resonating with intensity—how can a man make himself visible in a world that overlooks his existence? The answer, though left unaddressed by Sennett (1993), emerges from the desperation of invisibility—violence becomes the language of the unseen. The hidden injury of class, veiled in shame, looms large in their exploration, compelling them to assert that the remedy lies in dismantling the oppressive walls of shaming, paving the way for a society characterised by true classlessness.

Shame, a potent emotional force, emerges as the pivot upon which behavioural violence hinges. It is not absolute poverty or material lack that births shame; rather, it is the relative deprivation of dignity, self-respect, and pride. The chasm between the wealth of the elite and the meagre fortunes of the lower rungs wields immense power, fuelling feelings of inferiority and humiliation. Marx himself recognised that it was not the destitution of poverty that stung the spirit, but the stark proximity of hovels to opulent palaces. He understood shame as the driving emotion of revolution, empowering the poor to rise against their oppressors. Yet, a general rise in living standards or income, though promising, often fails to bridge the gap of shame. The improvement sets forth a revolution of rising expectations, kindling aspirations for equality that outpace tangible achievements.

The psychological landscape echoes with the voices of black communities, scarred by the wounds of racial discrimination. Frantz Fanon, a revolutionary black psychiatrist, bears the burden of shame and self-contempt in a world dominated by whites. His words, like haunting poetry, recount the disgrace of being black, rising burdened with the shame of colour.

Grier and Cobbs (1969), black psychiatrists, weave tales of an endless circle of shame, humiliation, and the perpetual sense of unacceptability experienced by many blacks. Kenneth Clark and Bancroft Clark (1989), distinguished black psychologists, delve into the emotional struggles of black individuals emerging from childhood marked by inferior treatment, highlighting how the stigma of inferiority lingers and rarely dissipates.

In this heart-rending tale of class and caste, the trajectory of violence emerges as a path paved with shame, woven into the fabric of society. The search for resolution lies not only in economic prosperity but in fostering true equality, a world where shaming finds no home, and violence is silenced in the embrace of collective dignity and self-worth. Only then can the shackles of shame be cast off, allowing each soul to stand tall, unburdened by the chains of violence.

Inferior social status not only fosters feelings of inferiority but also engenders a paradoxical sense of innocence. It is a psychological mechanism deeply rooted in the human psyche, where pain, punishment, and suffering play a dual role—intensifying feelings of shame while simultaneously relieving feelings of guilt and sinfulness.

As the pendulum of emotions swings, this intricate principle finds expression in various aspects of human life. It echoes in the realm of religion, where the act of penance seeks to relieve the burden of sin through self-inflicted pain and deprivation. The weight of wrongdoing is lightened as the soul embraces self-imposed penance, seeking redemption and solace.

In the halls of justice, the legal practice of punishment shares a similar intent. It endeavours to cleanse the soul of moral and legal guilt through the imposition of consequences. The act of punishment serves as a means to remove or undo the transgressions, offering a path to redemption and societal reconciliation.

Here, the essence of poverty finds its place in the tapestry of emotions—etymologically and psychologically intertwined with pain, punishment, and misery. It is a condition where the weight of hardship rests heavily upon the spirit, intensifying feelings of shame and inadequacy. Yet, beneath this shroud of adversity lies a paradoxical respite—the relief it brings from the burden of guilt and sinfulness. In the shadows of poverty, a sense of innocence emerges, not in the conventional sense, but rather as a counterbalance to the prevailing shame and humiliation. The experience of suffering and deprivation creates a narrative where one's struggles become a testament to the absence of wrongdoing. Poverty, by its very nature, speaks to the lack of opportunity and the imbalances that perpetuate inequality.

This dual nature of poverty, as both a bearer of shame and a dispenser of innocence, serves as a poignant reflection of the human condition. It is a paradox that beckons introspection and empathy, urging society to address the structural imbalances that bind individuals to their disadvantaged positions. Within this paradox lies a challenge for the collective conscience—to unveil the mechanisms that perpetuate poverty and dismantle the barriers to equality. By acknowledging the multifaceted nature of poverty, we open a gateway to transformative change, where suffering is not the arbiter of innocence, but where every soul finds solace and dignity in the embrace of compassion and equity. In this pursuit, the intricate dance between shame, guilt, and innocence reveals a path towards a more just and compassionate society.

CHAPTER 10

CLASSISM & THE SHAME OF POVERTY

"As long as poverty, injustice, and gross inequality persist in our world, none of us can truly rest."

- Nelson Mandela

In the realm of South Sudanese suffering, we have explored various forms of violence that have inflicted deep scars on the collective psyche. However, it is crucial to acknowledge that not all harm inflicted upon South Sudanese originates from direct attacks or interpersonal violence. Beyond the confines of privilege, many South Sudanese endure suffering due to the organization of society, the distribution of resources, and the perpetuation of inequalities. They experience unnecessary pain and are deprived of their lives prematurely. But can we label this as violence?

Consider the grim reality that while less than half a million people are intentionally killed every year across the world, a staggering nine million die due to starvation. The question then arises: Is this violence? Unlike the deliberate acts depicted in Kevin Carter's haunting image of a vulture and a little girl, these deaths are not the result of someone purposefully starving others to death. Yet, these traumas and deaths are preventable; they would not occur if we made different choices in how we distribute resources globally, ceased manufacturing weapons used in wars, and rejected divisive labels such as "FIRST world" and "THIRD world," "DEVELOPED" and "UNDERDEVELOPED," "LOWER CLASS," "MIDDLE CLASS," and "UPPER CLASS." Shockingly, eight hundred million people endure extreme poverty, and the astonishing fact is that just a fraction of international weapons spending could eradicate global poverty.

These insidious forms of harm are what we refer to as structural violence. However, labelling it as such challenges our traditional ways of thinking about violence or trauma. Suddenly, the focus shifts away from individual perpetrators, compelling us to explore new avenues to protect people from systemic harm.

An illuminating example of this theory of violence is found in the complex relationship between unemployment and violence. While there is a statistical correlation between the two, it is not a direct cause-and-effect relationship. The true trigger of violence is not mere unemployment but the profound loss of self-esteem and self-worth, the devastating blow to one's sense of adequacy and worthiness. This is especially poignant in cultures like South Sudan's patriarchal society, where men are expected to be providers. The shame induced by rejection, enforced passivity, and dependency precipitated by job loss and placement at the lowest socioeconomic spectrum can be overwhelming. It is important to note, however, that not everyone who experiences unemployment resorts to violence. The psychological impact of unemployment is shaped by individual strengths and vulnerabilities, as well as societal meanings attributed to it. The cultural response, both in economic terms and moral value judgments, plays a crucial role in shaping the psychological impact of unemployment on an individual.

In the context of South Sudanese society, manifestations of violence extend beyond direct physical aggression. Structural violence infiltrates the fabric of daily life, shaping the experiences of our people and leaving indelible wounds on their minds and bodies. By understanding and addressing these complex forms of harm and trauma, we can aspire to build a society where protection and compassion transcend traditional boundaries, fostering a more just and equitable world for all.

In the complex web of violence and its origins, shame emerges as a potent force that influences its hosts—the individuals who ultimately succumb to violent acts. But how does shame propagate, and through what channels does it permeate the hearts and minds of people? To understand this phenomenon, we must examine the intricacies of the social and economic system, where shame operates in two distinct ways, playing a pivotal role in the prevalence of violence.

Firstly, the social structure divides the population along vertical lines, creating a hierarchical ranking of individuals based on class, caste, race, age, and other criteria that segregate them into in-groups and out-groups, powerful and weak, rich and poor, honoured and dishonoured. Shame, in this context, operates systematically and wholesale, heightening vulnerability to feelings of humiliation among those assigned inferior social or economic status, such as South Sudanese refugees in the diaspora. The deeper the sense of inferiority and humility, the more frequent and intense the experience of shame, which, in turn, fuels acts of violence. The asymmetry of social roles, particularly gender roles, adds another dimension to this phenomenon. In patriarchal cultures, men and women face different expectations, and behaviours that lead to shame or honour differ for each gender. Men may be shamed for not displaying enough violence, being labelled as cowards or even facing death as deserters. Conversely, the more violent a man is, the more he is honoured with medals, promotions, and titles. Violence becomes a successful strategy for men to gain status and recognition.

The correlation between violence and poverty emerges as a significant factor in the prevalence of homicide rates worldwide. Numerous studies, such as those by Gebremikael (2003), Anser & Yousaf (2020), Dong, Egger & Guo (2020), and De Courson & Nettle (2021), have consistently found significant links between the degrees of absolute and relative poverty and the occurrence of homicide. Countries with the highest disparities in wealth and income, especially in the Third World regions of Latin America, Africa, and Asia, also exhibit the highest homicide rates, alongside collective and political violence. Similarly, in developed nations, the United States stands out with the highest levels of income and wealth inequality, closely associated with markedly elevated homicide rates compared to other First World countries, which boast the lowest levels of inequity and relative poverty.

In Australia, similar correlations have been observed between violence and relative poverty. Economists have employed wage inequity as a measure of income disparity between the rich and poor, revealing a close link between joblessness and delinquent behaviours, particularly among African, specifically South Sudanese, young offenders. These findings underscore the importance of understanding the systemic factors that perpetuate shame, violence, and the shame-infused cycle of poverty.

In unravelling the intricate web of shame and its relationship with violence and poverty, we must recognise that tackling these challenges requires a multifaceted approach—one that addresses both the vertical and horizontal divisions within society and strives to eliminate the disparities in income and wealth that fuel this destructive cycle. By promoting a more equitable and compassionate social and economic system, we can aspire to break free from the chains of shame and violence, offering hope for a brighter and more harmonious future for all.

In the complex tapestry of economic inequality and

unemployment, violence emerges as a poignant outcome, driven by the overwhelming burden of shame and the intensification of existing traumas. Our language itself provides a glimpse into the profound psychological impact of how we describe social strata. The terminology we use labels the poor as the "lower" or "humbler" classes, juxtaposed with the "superiority" and "pride" associated with the wealthy. These linguistic distinctions contribute to creating a hierarchical ranking within society, leaving those in lower positions feeling not only economically disadvantaged but also humiliated and inferior, thus magnifying their sense of shame which then serves as triggers for existing traumas.

The intertwined relationship between shame and violence is further reinforced by the rift between one's aspirations and their actual achievements. In societies where rigid caste or class hierarchies persist, the shame of poverty may be perceived as a consequence of misfortune rather than personal shortcomings. In such circumstances, individuals of lower social status may adopt an attitude of apathy, fatalism, and passivity, as they believe their position is predetermined and unchangeable— an example of this is the many South Sudanese fathers who move back home, believing there is no hope in staying in the west because the systems here are set in a way that proves they will "never make it". However, this passivity can evolve into a powerful catalyst for explosive violence, particularly when societies reject the notion that one's caste or class is immutable and instead embrace the idea that poverty is a result of an individual's inherent inadequacy—e.g., young men from this class taking from the rich by force through planned aggravated burglaries.

It is crucial to recognise that societal structures can shape how individuals perceive their worth and potential. In societies with deeply entrenched hierarchies, the shame associated with poverty might lead people to accept their situation without challenging the status quo or challenging it through the use of force—employing violence. But when societal norms shift, and people begin to question the legitimacy of such rigid divisions, the shame of poverty can transform into a driving force for change. The perception that poverty is not an inherent fate but rather a result of systemic flaws or injustices can ignite the flames of revolution and inspire collective movements to dismantle oppressive structures.

The complex interplay of shame, economic disparity, and violence cannot be viewed in isolation. It is a dynamic dance between the individual and society, where the feeling of humiliation due to social status can exacerbate traumas and pave the way for violent expressions of frustration and discontent. By delving deeper into the roots of these issues, we gain a better understanding of the human psyche's intricate workings and the mechanisms through which violence becomes entwined with economic inequality and unemployment. Addressing this entanglement requires not only addressing material disparities but also empowering individuals with a sense of agency and hope, helping them break free from the shackles of shame and envision a brighter future for themselves and their communities.

The Western social and economic system epitomises conditions that amplify shame and, consequently, violence. The pervasive "Horatio Alger" myth perpetuates the idea that anyone can become wealthy through intelligence and hard work, suggesting that failure to achieve wealth is a sign of stupidity or laziness. This constant stimulation to pursue wealth increases the frequency and intensity of feelings of shame, which, in turn, drives rates of violent crimes in our society.

The repercussions of unemployment are particularly significant. The loss of jobs and income often shatters self-esteem, and for some men, barely holding onto their self-worth even with stable employment, this can lead to violent outbursts when faced with joblessness. The societal equation of self-worth with net worth deepens feelings of inferiority and rejection among those who cannot secure or maintain a job while witnessing others' continued prosperity.

A real-life example showcases the harrowing impact of economic hardship on an individual. Amid the COVID-19 lockdown, a South Sudanese man grappled with unemployment and financial pressures. Despite his efforts to find work, his situation remained dire, and he relied on his family for support. The mounting shame over his inability to provide for his family reached a boiling point when an argument with his wife led her to question his masculinity. In a desperate bid to prove his manhood and counteract the emasculating shame, he resorted to violence and inflicted severe harm on his wife, ultimately leading to his arrest. When I spoke with the victim (his wife), she revealed the long suffering from financial constraints in their family and on their relationship. Though law enforcement agencies intervened by making an arrest and the perpetrator faced assault charges, they paid little to no attention to the connection between the family's financial pressures, exacerbated by the high number of job losses during COVID-19, and this family's experience of violence.

This tragic tale exposes the intensity of shame experienced by unemployed individuals and how it can drive them to extreme actions. The sense of failure and inadequacy can push some to conceal their struggles until the pressure becomes unbearable, culminating in destructive outbursts that leave a trail of devastation in their wake.

In summary, economic inequality and unemployment have deep-rooted connections to violence, as they amplify feelings of shame and exacerbate existing traumas. Understanding these complex dynamics is essential for addressing the roots of violence and crafting effective strategies to protect and support vulnerable individuals such as the South Sudanese community and other refugee migrants' families and communities in society.

In the complex social landscape, caste stratification inflicts a heavy toll on the Black community, giving rise to the emergence of violence, rooted in the very fabric of rejection, humiliation, and inferior treatment experienced by those in the lower castes. In this societal hierarchy, the upper castes wield their power to socially and vocationally exclude those considered beneath them, perpetuating a cycle of rejection and disdain. The impact of this discrimination is evident in various aspects of life, where blacks face challenges in housing, employment, and even their treatment compared to their white counterparts.

One striking manifestation of this caste-induced violence is the phenomenon of white flight, where whites vacate neighbourhoods upon the arrival of black residents. This act of fleeing from the presence of black individuals serves as a glaring symbol of the rejection and inferior treatment meted out to them. Moreover, the employment disparity between whites and blacks further compounds the situation, as blacks find themselves at the mercy of unequal opportunities, being the last to be hired and the first to be fired. This stark difference in employment rates continues to persist, leaving black citizens vulnerable to public humiliation and degradation in situations where their white counterparts would not face similar treatment.

The constant barrage of shaming and the ascription of inferiority endured by lower caste groups inevitably takes a toll on their sense of self-worth. They are made to feel shamed, insulted, disrespected, and dismissed, all stemming from the systematic mistreatment they have been subjected to, as echoed by their writers and leaders. Such experiences create a breeding ground for feelings of resentment and even rage. For those who lack non-violent means of restoring their personal dignity, violence may seem the only outlet for expressing their profound emotions. The burden of lower caste status brings forth a host of disadvantages, primarily stemming from the lack of equal access to lucrative careers, quality education, and vocational prospects. This glaring inequality in opportunities sets in motion a perpetual cycle of socioeconomic disparities, entrenching a system where those in the lower castes face significant challenges in improving their circumstances. Consequently, the rates of offending and violent crimes within lower-caste groups are alarmingly higher compared to their upper-caste counterparts, year after year.

The wide disparity in offending rates serves as a poignant indicator of the profound impact of caste stratification on the lives of those marginalized by discrimination. The scarcity of opportunities imposed upon them fuels feelings of frustration, desperation, and hopelessness, leading some individuals to resort to criminal acts as a means of survival or rebellion against the unjust system. The lack of access to better prospects not only stifles their potential for personal growth but also creates an environment ripe for the emergence of criminal behaviour.

Moreover, the stark contrast in offending rates becomes a clear reflection of the systematic disadvantages faced by lower-caste communities. While upper-caste groups might have access to better education, financial resources, and societal privileges, those in the lower castes find themselves trapped in a vicious cycle of limited opportunities and heightened vulnerabilities. This cycle perpetuates violence and criminality, as individuals may believe that violence is their only recourse to address their grievances or assert their worth in a society that continuously undermines their value.

The deeply rooted ramifications of caste stratification are evident in the stark disparities between these two groups, highlighting the urgent need for comprehensive reforms to eradicate this discrimination. To break this cycle of violence and socioeconomic disparities, it is imperative to implement measures that ensure equal access to education, job opportunities, and resources for all individuals, regardless of their social standing. By fostering an environment of equality and inclusivity, society can work towards dismantling the barriers that perpetuate caste-based discrimination and create a more just and harmonious community for all its members. Addressing the structural inequalities and providing pathways for upward mobility will not only uplift the lives of those in the lower castes but also foster a stronger, more cohesive society as a whole.

It is crucial to recognize that the impact of caste-based violence is not isolated to the individuals directly affected; it reverberates throughout the community, creating a systemic environment where violence becomes a manifestation of pent-up frustration and the struggle for dignity and equality. Addressing this issue requires a collective effort to dismantle the structural barriers that perpetuate caste discrimination and to foster an environment where every individual is valued, respected, and provided with equal opportunities for growth and advancement. Only through such transformative change can we pave the way for a society that transcends the boundaries of class and embraces the inherent worth and potential of all its members.

CHAPTER 11

TRAUMATISED MASCULINITIES SPAWN VIOLENCE

"It is easier to build strong children than to repair broken men."

- Frederick Douglass

The insidious assignment of inferior positions to certain individuals fosters a venomous brew of emotions—feelings of inferiority that simmer and eventually erupt into a cauldron of rage and violence. To unravel the enigma of why men are often more predisposed to violence than women, one must embark on a journey deep into the heart of our patriarchal culture. Here, highly asymmetrical gender roles are bestowed upon each sex from birth, threading their way throughout the fabric of their lives, woven into the very essence of their existence.

Within these gender roles lies the key to understanding the sinister connection between violence and masculinity. In the realm of traditional patriarchy, masculinity is inextricably intertwined with the expectation—nay, the demand—of violence under an array of well-defined circumstances: during times of war, in response to perceived personal insult, in defence of the family's honour when a female strays from societal norms, or even while participating in all-male combat sports. The very word "Virtus," from which the modern concept of "virtue" springs, harkens back to a time when courage on the battlefield was deemed the quintessential virtue—a virtue synonymous with masculinity. In the annals of ancient Rome, "Virtus" was more than just courage; it was the essence of manhood itself, where to be a man meant to be a soldier.

For the South Sudanese, manhood serves as the bedrock of behaviour and decision-making, neatly categorised by a set of characteristics and performances that affirm one's male identity. These characteristics, as well as the cultural pressures to conform to them, are explored in greater depth in my book 'South Sudanese Manhood and Family Crisis in the Diaspora.' Within its pages lie revelations that shed light on the intricate web of expectations that define what it means to be a man in our society.

The truth is, the paths to violence and aggression are paved by societal norms and expectations, woven into the very fabric of our lives. The assignment of roles and the rigid adherence to them become the crucible in which men's emotions are forged, entwined with shame, honour, and the burden of proving one's manhood in a culture steeped in war-like tendencies. If we are to address the cycle of family and domestic violence that plagues our society, we must first confront the root causes and liberate ourselves from the chains of antiquated gender norms. Only then can we aspire to forge a new path, one that embraces the full spectrum of human emotion and expression, transcending the limitations of gendered expectations and fostering a culture of empathy, understanding, and peace.

Addressing family and domestic violence requires a profound understanding of the moral codes underpinning the fabric of certain patriarchal cultures and subcultures. In these realms, norms are enforced through the sanctions of shame and honour, giving rise to what I term the "code of shame." Within this code, violence finds rationalisation, legitimacy, encouragement, and even command; it encounters neither prohibition nor inhibition. Conversely, the morality described as a "code of guilt"—one that prohibits actions such as killing and stealing—is an attempt at a therapeutic remedy, seeking to cure the propensity for violence stimulated by shame. While noble, this attempt, unfortunately, has not yielded the desired results.

Why has the guilt or shame approach not proved effective in quelling violence? Insights and analysis of violence and extreme trauma presented in this book may hold the answer. The problem lies in the fact that guilt alone or shame fails to dismantle the very motivational structure responsible for initiating violence: shame and its shame-motivated impulses. As psychologist James Gilligan (2001) aptly puts it, guilt-ethics merely redirects the violence generated by shame, often directing it inward towards the self. It does not serve to prevent or inhibit violence but instead alters its trajectory, while the underlying problem remains unsolved.

To view suicide as an alternative to addressing poverty, bullying, or mental health issues is no solution, as both forms of violence are equally lethal. Similarly, masochism cannot serve as a remedy for sadism, since both manifestations of pathology are equally destructive and painful. Merely advocating for more love and less shame and guilt is overly simplistic; what we truly need is to identify the conditions that enable equality to flourish without inhibition from shame or guilt. It is evident that both shame and guilt act as impediments to love. Shame prevents individuals from extending love to others, stemming from a deficiency of self-love and encouraging the withdrawal of affection from others to reserve it solely for oneself. Conversely, guilt inhibits self-love, or pride, often labelled as the deadliest of the seven deadly sins by Christian guilt-ethics. Guilt fuels self-hatred rather than self-love, convincing individuals that they are guilty and deserving of punishment, not reward.

Thus, if we approach violence as a public health and preventive medicine issue, we must explore the conditions that trigger shame and guilt on a socially and epidemiologically significant scale. Foremost among these conditions are relative poverty, race, age discrimination, traumas, and sexual asymmetry. To truly prevent violence, either externally or within families, we must embark on an agenda of political and economic reform. The most effective social policies to prevent violence aim to reduce the prevalence of shame and trauma. This involves diminishing the intensity of passive, dependent, and regressive wishes that fuel shame. In turn, these wishes must be gratified by nurturing and caring for each other, healing old wounds, and preventing circumstances that inflict further traumas, especially among the most vulnerable in society, starting from childhood when the need for love and care is most intense and essential. Only through a comprehensive approach that addresses the root causes of violence can we aspire to foster a society free from the destructive shackles of shame and guilt, where love can blossom unimpeded, and violence becomes but a distant memory.

Relative poverty, where poverty exists alongside wealth for certain groups while others remain deprived, has a far more potent effect in evoking shame, triggering traumas, and subsequently fostering violence, than an absolute level of poverty that may be higher but universally shared. Shame is a phenomenon that resides in the eyes of the observer, yet it is more likely to manifest when the one being observed is perceived as richer and more powerful than oneself. In the language of antiquated morality, this disparity is termed injustice; and though the world may have advanced in many aspects, the perception of injustice still lingers in the minds of most, often leading to feelings of shame, which in turn triggers trauma and eventually culminates in violence.

Approaching the issue from the standpoint of public health, the social psychology of shame, discrimination, and violence assumes a pivotal role in the realm of preventive psychiatry. The study of the causes and consequences of shame, along with its psychodynamic parameters, becomes an urgent focus of investigation, particularly in light of the potential existential threat of violence in a nuclear age and the persistently high rates of violence in the South Sudanese communities.

As we navigate the complex web of human emotions, traumas, and societal dynamics, understanding the link between shame, discrimination, and violence becomes a matter of paramount importance. Addressing these issues demands a holistic approach, encompassing both political and social reforms aimed at reducing the disparities that engender shame and fostering a more equitable and compassionate society. Only by dismantling the forces of shame and discrimination can we hope to break the cycle of violence and pave the way for a future where the seeds of peace, understanding, and harmony can flourish.

Frail Masculinities Bring Shame and Trigger Traumas

Frail masculinities often act as triggers for traumas, resulting in a deep sense of shame. Franz Boas, in his work "General Anthropology" (1944), shed light on the underlying motive behind this aggressiveness: the desire to obliterate feelings of shame and amplify feelings of pride and social prestige. Within this culture, shame is a potent force, with moral sanctions and authority perceived to emanate from others. Protecting oneself from experiences of shame and safeguarding the family's reputation become paramount objectives, driving individuals to great lengths.

Shame, in the South Sudanese context, is not only an internal feeling but is also keenly perceived as something that occurs before an audience, an external judge whose gaze scrutinizes one's perceived weaknesses, failures, and inferiorities. The culture is entwined with shaming those who deviate from societal expectations, exemplified by the admonition "don't bring shame into this family" when young people make significant life decisions.

In contrast, a guilt culture stems from an internalised conscience and the moral laws one imposes upon oneself. Violating these moral laws triggers feelings of guilt and sinfulness. Unlike shame, guilt can be relieved through exposure, leading guilt cultures to institutionalise the confession of sins as a means of moral absolution.

Why does the perceived source of moral sanctions influence the likelihood and direction of violent impulses? The answer lies in the motivation behind shame and guilt. Shame drives a deep desire to eliminate the painful feeling of shame, often leading to the elimination of others, as it is seen as emanating from them. While achievements can mitigate shame by eliciting admiration and respect, circumstances may hinder such achievements, leaving elimination as the perceived alternative.

Conversely, guilt motivates the desire to eliminate the

painful feeling of guilt, which may be perceived as emanating from the self. In extreme cases, this may manifest in self-destructive behaviour, such as suicide, particularly evident among South Sudanese young people in Australia.

Understanding these complex dynamics is crucial in addressing the deep-rooted issues of shame and guilt within the South Sudanese communities. By recognising the influence of cultural and social factors on these emotions, society can work towards building healthier and more supportive environments, where individuals can find pathways to healing, self-acceptance, and non-violent resolutions. Only through such compassionate and holistic approaches can we hope to create a future where shame and guilt no longer fuel violence and suffering.

Indeed, the interplay between punishment, shame, and guilt is a significant factor with profound implications for the impact of punitive measures on violent crime within a society. Punishment, by its very nature, tends to intensify feelings of shame, particularly when it is imposed publicly or focuses on humiliation and degradation. When individuals are publicly shamed through punitive actions, they experience a heightened sense of disgrace and humiliation, further exacerbating their feelings of shame. However, the same punitive measures can have a contrasting effect on feelings of guilt. Punishment, whether self-inflicted or imposed by others, can offer a form of atonement or reparation for perceived wrongdoings. It provides a mechanism for individuals to seek absolution and to alleviate their sense of guilt by paying for their actions through punishment.

These psychological nuances have important implications for how societies deal with violent crime. A punitive approach that heavily relies on shame-based tactics may inadvertently perpetuate cycles of violence, as individuals respond to their intensified feelings of shame by redirecting their anger and aggression towards others. The punitive actions, in this case, may further fuel the very violence they seek to address.

On the other hand, a more balanced approach that acknowledges the complexities of shame and guilt can foster a more nuanced response to violent crime. By addressing the root causes of violence, such as poverty, discrimination, trauma, and other societal issues, and by providing opportunities for healing and rehabilitation, societies can work towards breaking the cycle of violence. Furthermore, restorative justice practices that focus on repairing harm, promoting empathy, and fostering reconciliation between victims and offenders can be more effective in addressing the underlying issues that lead to violent behaviour. Such approaches prioritize healing and transformation over punitive retribution, offering a path towards healing for all parties involved.

As we delve deeper into the intricacies of punishment, shame, and guilt, it becomes evident that a one-size-fits-all approach to addressing violence may not yield the desired results. Instead, a comprehensive understanding of these psychological mechanisms is essential in crafting more effective and compassionate strategies to build safer, more harmonious societies. In the forthcoming chapter, a more in-depth exploration of these ideas will shed light on how societies can move towards a future where violence is addressed with empathy, healing, and prevention at its core.

The dynamics of shame, violence, and inequality form intricate and interconnected patterns within society, creating a web of "vicious circles" that perpetuate each other. To feel shamed is to experience a deep sense of disrespect, and individuals may respond to this perceived disrespect by seeking ways to gain respect through fear and intimidation. This false and costly form of respect arises when genuine respect and self-esteem are lacking, leading individuals to resort to aggression and violence to assert dominance and control. The feeling of shame is closely intertwined with the fear of ridicule, and individuals may resort to violent behaviour to halt laughter and replace it with tears. In the quest to avoid being the subject of mockery, some may resort to aggression as a means of silencing potential critics or rivals—we've seen this among young South Sudanese who go on to project their hurts onto their peers (the rise of knife crime in Victoria, among young people as a part of the lateral violence I discussed above).

Anthropological research has shed light on the relationship between shame and violence. Cultures that exhibit high levels of shame-related traits, such as boastfulness, sensitivity to insult, and ostentatious displays of wealth, are often more prone to engage in violence. The pursuit of military glory, warfare, violent crimes, and other aggressive behaviours are more prevalent in such cultures.

Furthermore, data from the Human Relations Area Files reveal that shame and violence are not only correlated with each other but also with measures of social and economic inequality. Cultures with hierarchical systems, such as social classes or caste systems, tend to experience higher levels of shame and violence compared to more egalitarian societies. Inequality exposes individuals to the risk of being perceived as inferior, leading to aggressive competition to impose inferior status on others, perpetuating the cycle of shame and violence.

In these complex feedback loops, shame stimulates violence and violence reinforces shame, while inequality fosters both shame and violence, creating a self-reinforcing cycle of destructive behaviour. Breaking free from these vicious circles requires a comprehensive approach that addresses the root causes of shame, guilt, and violence, including tackling issues of social and economic inequality.

By fostering genuine respect and self-esteem within individuals, and promoting social systems that prioritise equality and mutual support, societies can work towards dismantling these cycles of shame and violence. Understanding the intricate interplay of shame, violence, and inequality is crucial for developing effective strategies to build more compassionate and harmonious communities, where every individual can thrive without the need for aggression or fear.

CHAPTER 12

WOMEN VIOLENCE

In exploring the realm of women's violence, we must discern the stark contrasts in gender roles and their impact on shaping differing rates of violent behaviour. To comprehend the decisive difference between male and female gender roles, we delve into the circumstances that either augment or diminish shame and honour for individuals of each gender. Are these circumstances the same for both sexes, or do they diverge?

For South Sudanese women, the situation stands in stark contrast to that of men. Gender roles prescribe derogatory labels such as "slut," "whore," "bitch," or "tramp" exclusively for them, particularly in the context of marriage. In parallel, just as the term "cuckold" applies solely to men, "promiscuous" is predominantly used to shame women. However, what is most pertinent in this context is that women are not shamed for embodying traits of submissiveness, dependence, lack of aggression, or sexual inactivity or impotence, as men might be. Instead, they are shamed for possessing the very opposite characteristics: rebellion, independence, aggressiveness, and sexual activity. Therefore, if a woman responds to shame by becoming assertive or resorting to violence, she may face further shame rather than experiencing a reduction in violent tendencies. In patriarchal societies, such as the South Sudanese culture, violence among women is deemed "unfeminine," perpetuating a complex web of societal expectations.

In the context of the war in South Sudan, societal norms dictated that only men were expected (and either permitted or coerced) to participate in armed conflicts, while women were relegated to seeking refuge in neighbouring countries with their children. This convention has only recently begun to be questioned. The central implication of this gendered division is that, in patriarchal societies, men are assigned the role of "violence-objects," while women are confined to the role of "nurturing/caregiving." As a result, men are exclusively assigned the role of combatants, leaving them with no choice in the matter. Refusing to treat other men as objects of violence or declining to become violence-objects themselves would subject them to shame and insults, labelled as cowards and subsequently subjected to violence from their own army. A harrowing example of this was evident in the forcible removal of the Sudan Lost Boys from their homes without consent, compelling them to join the war against the Northern regime.

Consequently, in patriarchal societies, men are both shamed for refusing to treat others and themselves as violence-objects and honoured for their willingness to do so. This glorification of violence, especially in war contexts, creates a dangerous cycle that perpetuates a culture of aggression and dominance among men. These patriarchal structures leave both men and women as victims in their own sections of the divide, creating layered forms of violence experiences for all genders.

To understand and address the complexities of women's violence, we must critically examine and challenge the patriarchal norms that perpetuate rigid gender roles and exacerbate shame and honour dynamics. Breaking free from the confines of traditional gender expectations and promoting a more egalitarian society can pave the way for a more compassionate and peaceful coexistence, where both men and women are liberated from the chains of violence and discrimination. Only by collectively working to dismantle the underlying structures of patriarchal violence can we hope to foster a world where all individuals are free to express their true selves without fear of shame or prejudice.

In the intricate web of human societies, there exists a peculiar concept called "honour." It is a coveted prize, an accolade that is bestowed upon a select group of individuals—men. But what deeds are deemed worthy of such an esteemed recognition? Surprisingly, it is violence that earns men this revered honour, or more precisely, their ability to transform themselves and their fellow men into objects of each other's violence. I do not say this to cast shame upon those brave souls who have willingly sacrificed their safety and even their lives to protect their comrades-in-arms and defend the rest of us from the brutal violence inflicted on us by the civil war and by other men. Their valiant acts of courage deserve recognition and respect.

Instead, I highlight these facts to shed light on the underlying causes of male violence and to clarify why it is that most lethal violence is predominantly committed by men, and not as frequently or effectively by women. In a world where honour is synonymous with violence, where the embodiment of masculinity is intricately intertwined with dominance and aggression, men find themselves entangled in a paradoxical struggle. They must tread the thin line between being protectors and perpetrators, and the distinction can sometimes become blurred.

South Sudanese men, too, are subjected to societal pressures, expectations, and norms that dictate their worth based on their capacity to assert dominance and control, often through violence. The desire for recognition, respect, and affirmation of their masculinity fuels the cycle of violence, perpetuating the glorification of aggression and the suppression of vulnerability. This complex interplay of cultural conditioning, social and class structures, and patriarchal constructs forms the foundation upon which male violence is rooted.

Conversely, South Sudanese women, burdened with the weight of entirely different gender roles, do not frequently find honour through acts of violence. Their femininity is often associated with nurturing and care, and they are not expected or encouraged to resort to violence as a means of asserting their worth. Instead, women navigate a different set of challenges, often fighting against the constraints imposed upon them by patriarchal norms.

To understand and address the deeply entrenched issue of male violence, we must peel back the layers of societal conditioning and explore the multifaceted factors contributing to this phenomenon. By challenging traditional notions of masculinity, promoting empathy, emotional intelligence, and non-violent conflict resolution, we can begin to pave the path toward a more compassionate and equitable world. A world where honour is redefined, no longer confined to the shadows of violence, but embracing the true essence of humanity—the capacity to love, care, and uplift one another. Only through a collective effort to challenge the status quo and dismantle harmful gender stereotypes can we hope to create a society where both men and women are liberated from the chains of violence and bestowed with the true honour of fostering peaceful families and communities.

Single-Parent Families

In the intricate tapestry of the South Sudanese community, another thread that weaves intricately with the rates of violence, particularly in the diaspora, is the prevalence of single-parent families. Indeed, numerous studies have illuminated the correlation between growing up in single-parent households and the increased likelihood of facing various adversities (Stritzel et al., 2021; Demuth & Brown, 2004). The research consistently highlights that children raised in single-parent families are more vulnerable to experiencing abuse, engaging in delinquent behaviours, and eventually getting entangled in criminal activities compared to their counterparts raised by both parents (Sampson & Laub, 1994). These findings shed light on the critical impact of family structure on the development and well-being of children.

Over the past three decades, a significant and concerning trend has emerged: the simultaneous rise in violent crime rates and the prevalence of one-parent families (Manning & Lamb, 2003; Manning & Brown, 2023). This parallel increase suggests an interconnected relationship between these two factors within the South Sudanese communities. As the number of single-parent families has grown, so has the occurrence of youth violence, hinting at a possible association between the two phenomena. While this correlation does not necessarily imply causation, it raises important questions about the potential influence of family structure on the development of violence within the community.

Certain theorists have posited that the surge in youth violence in recent years could, at least in part, be attributed to the increasing prevalence of single-parent families (McLanahan & Sandefur, 1994). This hypothesis draws attention to the multifaceted nature of the issue, acknowledging that family structure is only one among many contributing factors. Nonetheless, it emphasises the significance of understanding and addressing the challenges faced by single-parent households in the South Sudanese communities, who are potentially parenting while dealing with their own traumas.

As a woman who was raised by a single parent myself, I acknowledge the challenges that come with raising a child single-handedly. Parenting is an intricate and demanding task that necessitates all the support one can get, and having two caring and responsible parents undoubtedly lightens the burden. Notably, children, especially boys, can greatly benefit from having a positive male role model within the household or community, which has been shown to reduce the risk of delinquency and violent criminal tendencies.

In South Sudanese single-parent families, it is often the father who is noticeably absent. Criminologists have observed that countries like Japan and Sweden, where the rates of one-parent families are lower, also exhibit lower rates of youth male offending.

Undoubtedly, economic advantage plays a significant role in fostering a positive environment for parenting and social activities that are crucial for the healthy development of children and young individuals (Duncan & Brooks-Gunn, 2000). Economic stability within a household can alleviate stress levels and provide parents with the resources and opportunities to support their children's emotional, educational, and recreational needs (Yoder, Brisson & Lopez, 2016). A nurturing environment, bolstered by economic well-being, reduces the likelihood of risky behaviours and negative interactions with peers that could otherwise serve as risk factors for delinquency and involvement with the justice system. Having an economically nurtured environment can reduce triggering stressors South Sudanese single-parents experience.

However, to comprehensively address the issue of violence within the South Sudanese communities, we must avoid oversimplification and recognise the complex interplay of multiple factors at play. The root causes of violence are deeply intertwined with broader political, social, economic, traumas, environment, and cultural realities that demand thoughtful consideration. While economic stability is undeniably vital, it cannot be viewed in isolation from other societal aspects that contribute to violence and inequality.

To effectively combat violence, we must adopt a multi-faceted approach that extends beyond merely supporting single-parent families. Addressing economic inequality, limited access to opportunities, and the absence of robust social support systems must be integral parts of our strategy. Societal change necessitates collective efforts to dismantle the structures that perpetuate inequity and disempowerment.

By working together to create a more equitable and inclusive society, we can lay the groundwork for a brighter future where every child has the chance to flourish, irrespective of their family structure. Such a collective effort entails providing opportunities for education, job training, and equitable employment to empower families across the community. It also involves fostering healing initiatives and programs that can address underlying traumas. By bolstering social support networks, we can offer both parents and children the resources and guidance needed to thrive in a nurturing environment.

Only through a holistic and collaborative endeavour can we hope to mend the frayed threads of the community's fabric and weave a new tapestry of peace, understanding, and prosperity for generations to come. This vision requires fostering a culture of empathy, compassion, and mutual respect, where all individuals are valued for their unique contributions to society. By tackling violence at its roots and building an inclusive community, we pave the way for a brighter future. In this future, the potential of every South Sudanese individual can truly be realised, and we can fully heal to avoid traumatic outbursts that lead to devastating events.

CHAPTER 13

FILICIDE

"It is very tempting to take the side of the perpetrator. All the perpetrator asks is that the bystander do nothing. He appeals to the universal desire to see, hear, and speak no evil. The victim, on the contrary, asks the bystander to share the burden of pain. The victim demands action, engagement, and remembering."

- Judith Herman

The concept of a continuum of violence against women was developed and associated with Surviving Sexual Violence by Liz Kelly (1988). Kelly's concern was to change the standard approach from categorising violence against women and girls

(VAWG) as episodic and deviant incidents (defined in law as crimes) of extreme cruelty and harm to recognising that it is normative and functional: an everyday context for the lives and experiences of women and girls all over the world. However, in the context of this chapter, I will go beyond VAWG and include the variety of violence to show how these continuing experiences of violence shape, reshape and result in a mothers act of extreme violence against her own children. How traumatic experiences among the South Sudanese women such as Akon who murdered her own children and who's case-study I will explain and analysis momentarily stems from a place of prolong suffering and victimisation. I argue in this chapter that, although there are continuing multiple forms of violence experienced by South Sudanese women, they are interrelated: they define a continuum from trivial to extreme violence. Violence against oneself, interpersonal violence, communal violence, structural violence, and civil wars. Another continuum is its spiral development, with violence generating violence and pushing it to grow. Violence can also be learned, which makes progress ever further in violence: in families, in communities, in armies, and society (Miller & Knudsen, 2007). Continuing experiences of violence can leads to many forms of traumatic experiences in ones and or in collective lives.

A horrifying act of violence that resulted in a murder of young children by their mother In Melbourne Australia I will use as a case study is that of Akon Goud. Anyone who was in Australia or had access to the internet in April 2015 was touched by the tragic loss of innocent lives: Akon Goud's children, her 16-month-old son Bol, and four-year-old twins Hanger and Madit, whom she drove into a lake with her daughter Alual, who survived, in Wyndham Vale, Melbourne, Victoria, Australia.

In the sombre April of 2015, a heart-wrenching tragedy unfolded in an Australian suburb. The nation watched in shock as Akon Goud, a grief-stricken mother, drove her innocent children—16-month-old Bol and four-year-old twins Hanger and Madit—into the cold embrace of a lake in Wyndham Vale, a suburb in the Western part of Melbourne, Victoria, Australia. Only her daughter Alual survived, spared from the terrible fate that befell her siblings. This heart-wrenching incident captured the attention of media outlets, academics, and independent writers alike, each seeking to unravel the enigma of this sorrowful event. The community watched the news in despair as the alleged murder case unfolded in the media.

In the aftermath of the tragedy, as the wheels of justice turned, Akon found herself in the clutches of the law at Southern Cross Train Station in Melbourne, Victoria, on the day of her arrest. As an interpreter, I accompanied three seasoned detectives, two males and one female, as we embarked on the difficult task of understanding the untold depths of despair that led to this unimaginable act. Amid friendly banter and casual conversations, the detectives discussed their roles, sharing their wisdom and encouragement for my studies in criminology. Little did they know the gravity of the emotions awaiting us, emotions that defied simple explanations in English terms.

Initially, our intention was for me to listen to the phone calls Akon made before the tragic incident, hoping to decipher the puzzle of her motives. However, fate had other plans, and new developments led us on a journey to the countryside, where Akon was believed to be staying with her aunt after driving the children into the lake. As we traversed the road to the countryside, thoughts swirled in my mind—thoughts about the complex web of human emotions that drive such profound actions. The media frenzy outside the station mirrored the confusion inside, as journalists eagerly awaited the unfolding of events, hoping to capture the elusive essence of the truth.

Inside the station, the female detective prepared the interview room with meticulous care, ensuring every moment was captured through video and audio recordings. As the door opened, Akon entered the room, her demeanour a tapestry of emotions—overwhelmed, disoriented, and sorrowful. As an interpreter, I chose to tread carefully, not wishing to reopen the wounds that haunted her soul. Our conversation remained measured, brief pleasantries exchanged as Akon grappled with the weight of her circumstances. Her silence spoke volumes, echoing the immense burden she carried within.

In a rare moment of vulnerability, she asked a poignant question when the female detective stepped out briefly, *"Are they going to put me in jail now? I need to call my family from Africa."* Her plea resonated with the uncertainty that lay ahead, as she awaited the detectives' questions and the unknown path that lay before her.

The tragic case of Akon Goud serves as a sombre reminder

of the multifaceted nature of human emotions and the need for a compassionate and comprehensive approach to understand and address violence within the South Sudanese community and alike communities from extreme war-torn nations. It sheds light on the hidden wounds that can fester beneath the surface, propelling individuals toward unimaginable actions. In this quest for understanding, we are reminded of the fragility of the human psyche and the importance of weaving a tapestry of empathy, support, and understanding to heal the wounds that haunt our communities.

In the dimly lit interview room, the weight of sorrow hung heavily in the air as Akon, the grieving mother, sat beside me, and the detective on the other side. The room, adorned with sophistication, featured a small coffee table between us, while a large video screen on the wall captured every moment of this harrowing encounter. The recording equipment was discreetly positioned, ensuring our voices were captured effortlessly and unobtrusively. The gravity of the situation necessitated formalities, and we began by introducing ourselves, declaring our names and roles in this tragic tale.

As the interview unfolded, the room echoed with Akon's tears and sobs, her heart-wrenching pain seeping into the very fabric of the space. She recounted the events leading to that fateful moment when she drove her car into the cold depths of the lake, a moment of unimaginable despair that would haunt her forever. The detective delved into every aspect, seeking to understand the motive that led to such a devastating decision. The video footage from her street provided a visual narrative, an eerie glimpse into the moments before her life unravelled irrevocably.

As the hours stretched on, exhaustion and hunger settled in, both for us and for Akon. Yet, the pursuit of answers pressed on relentlessly. In the words of Erich Maria Remarque, her mind had become a "soundless apparition," grappling with the weight of lived trauma and memories that refused to fade. Akon's mind was a labyrinth of experiences, from the horrors of war back home to the days leading up to the tragedy that shattered her world. As I interpreted her words, a profound question surfaced in my mind - do the emotions borne from trauma become an intrinsic part of one's identity? Trauma rips apart the very fabric of an individual's being, tearing away the layers that once bestowed respect, dignity, and self-worth. In Akon's case, the emotions of anger, resentment, and deep sorrow now inhabited the void left by the loss of her loved ones. They were on one hand as the fragments that remained, shaping her identity as a grieving mother but, on the other hand, as an alleged murderer.

Letting go of these emotions meant relinquishing the only connection she had to her lost loved ones, leaving her feeling exposed and vulnerable. In her fragile state, she oscillated between wiping away tears and wearing a distant smirk, as if retreating into a world that only she could comprehend. It was a coping mechanism, a way to navigate the emotional labyrinth that now defined her existence. In the poignant hours that followed, Akon's emotions became the haunting melody of her trauma, weaving a tapestry of loss and despair that words alone could not convey. Her shattered identity clung to these emotions, for they were now the remnants of a life once whole, now fragmented by a heart-wrenching tragedy. As I bore witness to this deeply wounded soul, the room seemed to hold its breath, acknowledging the weight of her grief.

In the silence that followed, the room stood as a testament to the complexities of human emotions, the echoes of a life forever changed by unimaginable loss. And as the night wore on, Akon's heartache remained, etched into the very essence of her being, a wounded mother who carried the weight of grief and loss as she faced the uncertain road ahead.

The room was shrouded in the darkness of the night, a midnight hour that seemed to stretch on endlessly. Akon sat beside me, her tears flowing like an unyielding river, each word she spoke accompanied by heart-wrenching sobs. The detective, her voice laced with frustration, fired questions one after another, seeking answers that could unravel the enigma of this tragic event. As the interpreter, I felt like a conduit for their emotions, a channel that bore the weight of their anguish and fury. The room seemed to close in on us, suffocating us with the weight of Akon's pain and the detective's relentless pursuit of truth—all she needed was a confession, perhaps a plea of guilt.

Hours seemed to blur into each other, the passage of time marked only by Akon's ceaseless tears and the detective's unyielding inquiries. It was an emotional turmoil, draining every ounce of strength from us, like a pipe channelling a relentless fire that threatened to consume everything in its path. As the night wore on, the room bore witness to the unfolding tragedy, an intricate dance of emotions and raw human experience.

A much-needed break finally arrived, offering respite from the overwhelming intensity of the interview. I reached out to my agency over the phone to inform them that the assessment had been completed, marking the longest and most emotionally taxing assignment in the company's history. My exhaustion was palpable, but there was little time for rest as the two male detectives offered to drop me off at my car.

As we emerged from the underground parking lot, the media's relentless pursuit continued, their lenses trained on us, hungry for a glimpse of Akon. The detective swiftly defended my presence, ensuring that their lens did not capture me as Akon but as a fellow officer of justice. The weight of the moment was heavy, and I instinctively shielded my face, seeking protection from the probing eyes of the media.

Silent contemplation filled the car as we made our way to my parked vehicle. The detectives once again broached the subject of Akon's case, curious about cultural perspectives and insights. Yet, I held steadfast to my role as an interpreter, refusing to offer opinions that went beyond my mandate. It was not that I didn't have a cultural opinion on the circumstance that might have played a role in Akon's decision, but for women like Akon, a cultural aspect is just a drop in the ocean of their intersecting traumatic circumstances. If I were to voice an opinion, where would I even start, and do these detectives have enough time to fully listen and comprehend Akon's as well as our community's experiences, I asked myself. Their persistence faded, and as the car rolled to a stop, they presented a unique opportunity—a chance to work with Victoria Police.

Their words left me pondering the possibilities, a journey that was not part of my plans but held undeniable allure. As we bid each other farewell, I couldn't help but be touched by the genuine concern and camaraderie of the detectives. Their offer remained a seed planted in my mind; a possibility that could bloom into something unforeseen.

As I drove away, the echoes of the night's events resonated within me, a tapestry woven with the threads of sorrow and resilience. The encounters with Akon and the detectives had left an indelible mark, reminding me of the complexities of human emotions and the weight of the justice system's burden. As the night turned into a new day, I was left with a sense of gratitude for having borne witness to this profound human experience, even in its darkest moments, as well as a feeling of extreme worry for what lies ahead for Akon and any other South Sudanese mother struggling with our past and current circumstances in the West.

As the sun began to rise on the horizon, painting the sky with hues of pink and orange, a sense of both uncertainty and anticipation filled the air. The events of the previous night had left me introspective, my mind racing with thoughts about the path that lay ahead. There was an undeniable shift within me, a newfound purpose awakened by the profound encounters with Akon and the detectives. The night's conversations and emotions had stirred a spark of curiosity deep within my soul, igniting a desire to delve deeper into the intricacies of human behaviour and the justice system. The detectives' offer to work with Victoria Police had opened a door to a realm of possibilities, challenging me to consider a future that I had not envisioned before.

As I drove through the streets, the city awakening around me, I couldn't help but feel a sense of awe at the vastness of life's tapestry. The road ahead was uncharted, its twists and turns a testament to the unpredictability of life's journey. Yet, there was a sense of excitement in the air, a feeling that each step I took would lead me closer to unravelling the mysteries that surrounded me. The promise of possibilities beckoned, like a distant beacon of light guiding me through the darkness. I knew that the future held challenges and uncertainties, but I was ready to embrace them with a newfound determination. The night's events had left an indelible mark on my heart, reminding me of the fragility of life and the resilience of the human spirit.

As I pondered the interplay of life's tragedies and triumphs, I realised they were like intertwined threads in a grand tapestry. Each thread contributed to the fabric of our existence, weaving together moments of sorrow and joy, pain and healing. It was in these intricacies that the beauty of life resided, in the harmony of contrasting experiences. The future held both uncertainty and possibility, but I was determined to embrace it with an open heart and an eager mind. The events of that night had given me affirmation and a renewed sense of purpose and a deeper appreciation for the complexities of human emotion. I was ready to step into the unknown, to navigate the uncharted waters of life, knowing that each step would be a dance between challenges and opportunities.

As the day unfolded before me, I couldn't help but wonder how the threads of my journey would intertwine with the grand tapestry of life. The possibilities were endless, and I was eager to explore every avenue that lay before me. With each passing moment, I felt a growing sense of excitement and curiosity, knowing that every twist and turn would shape the person I was to become. In the dance of life, tragedies and triumphs would intertwine, creating a symphony of experiences that would colour the canvas of my existence. The road ahead may be uncertain, but I was ready to embrace the journey, guided by the lessons of the night and the promise of a future filled with wonder and discovery.

And so, with a heart full of hope and a mind filled with curiosity, I embarked on the next chapter of my life, knowing that the dance of life's tragedies and triumphs would lead me to places I had never imagined. As I navigated the streets, I couldn't help but smile, for I knew that the journey ahead would be a testament to the resilience of the human spirit and the beauty of life's intricate dance.

As I stepped into the quiet sanctuary of my home, the weight of the night's emotional turmoil clung to my soul like a heavy shroud. The stillness enveloped me, wrapping me in a cocoon of solitude as I moved with hushed steps, careful not to disturb my mother's peaceful sleep. In the dim light, I tiptoed into the bathroom, seeking refuge from the haunting images of the criminal cases that had unfolded before my eyes. The water cascaded down like a gentle waterfall, cleansing my body but unable to wash away the lingering traces of pain and suffering etched in my mind.

Exhaustion bore down on me like a leaden weight, yet sleep eluded me like a playful phantom. Instead, my mind wove a tapestry, intricately connecting the threads of these cases, seeking to reveal the common thread that bound them together. The mosaic of suffering and sorrow played out before my eyes like a heart-wrenching drama, leaving me both captivated and tormented by the puzzle before me.

In this mental labyrinth, a revelation emerged like a brilliant sunrise, casting light upon the deeper layers of trauma that scarred our community, families, and lives. Like veterans returning from the battlefield, we bore the invisible wounds of our past, haunting reminders of the wars we endured. Akon, like many women in our community, carried the silent burden of war's aftermath - loss, instability, and psychological turmoil.

Our trauma ran deep, severing the threads that wove our relationships together, leaving us vulnerable to the cruel winds of life. Our sense of self fractured, like a shattered mirror reflecting distorted images of who we once were. The pain we carried hindered our ability to trust, to connect, and to find solace in the warmth of human bonds. Bessel van der Kolk's words resonated like an ancient prophecy, affirming that trauma's residue lingered within us, distorting our perceptions and shaping our responses to the world. It became a lens through which we viewed life, influencing our actions and guiding our footsteps. The scars of our past trauma coloured our interactions with ourselves and others, leaving us struggling to find harmony in a world riddled with brokenness.

Our community bore the weight of this collective trauma, impacting not just individuals but shaping the very fabric of our society. Like a stone thrown into a tranquil pond, the ripples of trauma extended far beyond the individual, touching every aspect of our existence. Our understanding of the complex interplay between trauma and behaviour offered a more nuanced perspective on the human experience. It posed questions not only about our past but also about who we were at present and how our collective trauma continued to shape our lives. By acknowledging this profound interconnection, we opened the door to healing, compassion, and empathy. The wounds of trauma ran deep, but in recognising its lasting effects, we embarked on a journey to build a more supportive and understanding community. It was a path that demanded courage, compassion, and a shared determination to mend the frayed threads of our existence.

As we navigated through life's tragedies and triumphs, we aspired to weave a tapestry of resilience, hope, and a more connected future. In this shared endeavour, we reached out to one another, extending a helping hand to those burdened by the weight of trauma, and together, we sought the light of healing amidst the darkness.

As I left Australia a couple of days after interpreting for Akon, my heart and mind were heavy with the burden of the case. During my travels abroad, I couldn't escape the haunting echoes of Akon's story, reverberating through media reports, colleagues, family, and friends. Almost everyone in our community discussed the case, and the entire nation of Australia was touched by the tragedy of three innocent, beautiful children losing their lives at the hands of their mother, the very person meant to protect them against all the ills of the world.

Despite being abroad, news of the case seemed to relentlessly find me, driving me to follow every media update closely, read every article on the case, and watch every televised court appearance. The incident intensified the already prevalent media spotlight on South Sudanese youth crimes and community issues. Amidst the discussions, there were intense scrutiny and questioning of the community, her ex-partner, and her family for potential shortcomings in supporting Akon, especially during her struggles with postpartum stress disorder after giving birth.

Many attempted to answer why Akon "broke," proposing numerous theories often focusing solely on gender and cultural factors. However, having worked closely with our community, it became evident that the answer to this complex question was far from straightforward. Gender aside, Akon's journey was a culmination of various grim circumstances she endured, both before and after settling in Australia. The tragic incident that led to the loss of her children was, in a sense, the last straw on the camel's back.

Yet, amidst the search for easy answers, the truth revealed itself as a tapestry woven with countless threads of pain and suffering. While people sought to understand why Akon reached her breaking point, the reality was that she had been broken by the traumas she experienced throughout her life, from the civil war to the challenges of resettlement. The weight of generational violence and trauma loomed over our community, affecting not just mothers like Akon but also fathers grappling with their psychological struggles, with some choosing to disappear.

Akon faced her trial, and after pleading guilty to charges of murder, infanticide, and attempted murder, she was sentenced to 26 and a half years in prison. Her case sparked a public outcry and multiple appeals, revealing the countless traumatic incidents she endured as a refugee. As her legal team, psychiatrists, and psychologists fought for a reduced sentence, hope emerged.

Upon my return, I resumed my work and research on family violence in the South Sudanese communities. One day, I received a booking to visit the Dame Phyllis Frost Centre in Ravenhall. Arriving early, I met a high-profile professional from the criminal justice system who guided me through security protocols. As we approached the ward where I was to meet Akon, friendly women doing gardening greeted me, a reminder of the humanity within the prison walls.

As we entered the interview room, the gravity of the case was palpable. Akon's story had become a turning point for her and our community, a reminder of the profound impact of trauma and the urgent need for healing. The road ahead was uncertain, but through empathy and compassion, we could strive to break the cycle of violence and suffering.

When Akon entered the room, her face lit up upon recognising me. Our warm exchange in Dinka signalled a missed connection since our first encounter. During the interview, my client asked Akon questions about her life, war experiences, and settlement in Australia. Tears flowed freely, and I found myself not just interpreting her words but also channelling her emotions. Akon, like many trauma victims, struggled to find adequate words to describe her experiences, highlighting the paradox of language during our conversation.

As the interview progressed, my client posed crucial questions to Akon to thoroughly understand her circumstances, her life back home, her experiences during the war, and her settlement in Australia. Tears flowed freely, punctuated by pauses as she sought words for her emotions. I found myself not just interpreting her words but also channelling her emotions, trying to convey the depth of her feelings within the constraints of language. Like many trauma survivors, Akon struggled to adequately express her experiences, highlighting the paradox of language during our conversation.

Language, while a potent tool for communication, also introduces a gap between the speaker and the traumatic event they attempt to convey. Akon's narrative, limited by language, seemed inadequate for encapsulating her experiences' true depth. This dilemma—how to articulate the inexpressible, how to share a truth when words fall short—is common among survivors. Despite her efforts, the full impact of the traumatic events eluded language's grasp.

In the backdrop of South Sudan's tumultuous past, where

sensory disruptions were routine, memories of trauma often merged, blurring past and present distinctions. The trauma narratives carried by victims and survivors went beyond mere details; they reflected the profound impact of those events on their lives. For them, trauma became a reference point, influencing their current experiences and emotions, a reality not fully captured by mere facts.

As Akon shared her experiences, I was transported to her reality, the refugee camp of hardship and violence, reminiscent of my family's experiences. Despite differing origins, her stories echoed mine, invoking vivid recollections of our shared history. Akon's narrative, with its fluid use of tense, transcended grammatical conventions, illustrating trauma's enduring pain. She felt powerless, mourning the loss of her children, father, and husband, with only time to potentially dull her grief.

Following our initial meeting, we reconvened weeks later, revisiting a world marked by sorrow. As Akon voiced doubts about her story's credibility and her children's reunion, she sought my perspective, hopeful. I reassured her with honesty, acknowledging the uncertainty but affirming her case's diligent handling. Her tearful smile expressed gratitude for the reassurance.

As the security guard escorted Akon back, the shared stories' weight resonated with me, highlighting the responsibility of interpreting others' trauma. Her narrative, a vivid reminder of trauma's lasting effects, underscored the need for empathy and understanding. Departing the prison, Akon's voice and her pain stayed with me, compelling me to advocate for healing, justice, and compassion. We must look beyond the surface, the visible acts of violence, to grasp the complex realities of refugees settling in new lands.

Exiting the room, my client and I carried our experiences differently; she with her comprehensive folder of notes, and I with only my lanyard, having left everything else behind. Our walk to the front office, where our belongings awaited, was marked by warm goodbyes and compliments from the women we passed. Stepping out of the prison's confines, we paused in the parking lot, reflecting on the emotional depth of Akon's story. My client, visibly moved, sought further insight from me, given my early involvement with Akon and our shared community background. This deep personal and professional connection to Akon's journey underscored the profound link between our experiences, emphasizing the critical role of empathy and understanding in addressing trauma.

In response to my client's query regarding Akon's case, I refrained from providing a standard, impersonal response, choosing instead to speak from the heart. To me, Akon was not merely a perpetrator; she was a woman who had faced immense hardships throughout her life, both in her homeland and as a migrant. She had endured the horrors of war, the loss of her spouse, and the challenges of motherhood under great adversity, parenting single-handedly in a foreign land. In my view, Akon's actions stemmed not from inherent malice but from a breaking point reached when her mental and emotional resilience was overwhelmed. Her story is a testament to a harrowing journey of trauma, loss, and the unbearable weight of her experiences. No punishment could restore her children, her sense of self, or her mental health. Our criminal justice system, while necessary for most cases, lacks a trauma-informed approach for individuals like Akon, leading to a uniformed method of addressing law, order, crime, and punishment. My empathy and compassion for Akon surpassed any feelings of judgment or condemnation. My client, understanding the complexity of Akon's life and the factors leading to such a tragic outcome, encouraged me to write about these issues. "Please, you must write about these matters. We know so little about the South Sudanese or their backgrounds," she said. Recognizing the widespread violence and trauma, she believed my writings could illuminate the lives of those deeply afflicted. We continued discussing trauma, war, interpersonal violence, and refugee communities in the parking lot for a few more minutes.

Driving home, Akon's words and the burden of her story stayed with me. The court's scrutiny and the 2018 appeal resulted in a reduced sentence, acknowledging her disturbed mental state at the incident's time. Her sentence was adjusted to 18 years, with a minimum of 14. Although this reduction provided some solace, I pondered Akon's future post-release. The scars of her experiences, haunting memories, and the consequences of her actions would persist. I contemplated the support she would need to rebuild her life and heal from her trauma.

Akon's case underscores the persistent effects of trauma and the importance of approaching human suffering with compassion. It challenges us to reflect on the complexities of human experience and the necessity of understanding and support for those enduring unimaginable pain. As I pursue my work and research, I aim to enhance awareness of trauma's lasting impact on individuals and communities. Akon's story, leaving a profound impression on my heart, emphasized the significance of empathy and the need for healing for those who have faced the depths of human tragedy.

In the Western world, a hopeful trend towards healing emerges, advocating for non-traditional psychiatric methods tailored to the unique circumstances of individuals, groups, and communities. These approaches promise relief from the ongoing turmoil caused by collective wounds. This evolution in treatment might allow us to comprehend and mitigate the suffering underlying such tragedies, identifying the essential needs for love, care, and respect as crucial for survival. Acknowledging signs of distress, from suicidal tendencies to psychological assessments, and from institutional escapes to community support, we might carve a route towards recovery.

Within the tumult of war, civilians, particularly women, face heightened vulnerability to psychological impacts. Both genders endure distinct traumas during conflict, each with differing psychological responses and coping mechanisms. War inflicts both acute and chronic health issues, with women facing violence even beyond their homes. In conflicts around the globe, women experience firsthand the horrors of war and harassment even in supposed refuges like refugee camps.

Women like Akon, departing war-afflicted regions, endure additional adversities on their journey to safety.

Within the tumult of war, civilians, particularly women, face heightened vulnerability to psychological impacts. Both genders endure distinct traumas during conflict, each with differing psychological responses and coping mechanisms. War inflicts both acute and chronic health issues, with women facing violence even beyond their homes. In conflicts around the globe, women experience firsthand the horrors of war and harassment even in supposed refuges like refugee camps. Women like Akon, departing war-afflicted regions, endure additional adversities on their journey to safety.

Amidst the unforgiving chaos of war-torn South Sudan, women bear the world's weight upon their shoulders. With their husbands lost to the abyss of conflict, they are thrust into unfamiliar roles, grappling with newfound responsibilities while their futures remain uncertain. Their burden extends far beyond their families, as they strive to rebuild shattered lives and dreams. Yet, the struggle for survival leaves them without the means to support their loved ones, forcing them to find solace in inadequate social welfare offerings. In the devastation's shadows, their cries echo through the void, their pain manifesting as somatic complaints, for the psychological roots of their suffering are unknown to them. Their silent struggle is veiled by the stigma that society casts upon mental health issues. These courageous souls navigate unstable paths with limited psychotherapy knowledge, and a world that turns a blind eye to their plight.

The chains of cultural norms and societal expectations further shackle women. They find themselves ensnared in strict social controls, confined to traditional roles that suffocate their dreams and aspirations. For widows, life becomes a relentless scrutiny of their actions, every step weighed against the expectations of a society steeped in patriarchal traditions. Meanwhile, widowers roam freely, their freedom untouched by the same scrutinising eyes. In the realm of post-war healing, therapists walk a tightrope, balancing respect for their clients' cultural values while empowering women to reclaim their voices and assertiveness. Yet, this delicate dance of cultural sensitivity comes with a caveat: the therapists from an individualistic society confront the reality that the women they seek to help come from communal societies, where one's role defines their entire existence. Healing must transcend individual pain to address the collective trauma that permeates their lives.

For women like Akon, the struggle is a symphony of past traumas and current stressors, intertwining to compose a heart-wrenching symphony of suffering. They bear war scars on their bodies and unimaginable grief in their hearts. In their eyes, we glimpse the unspoken pains of countless women, etched in calamity's shadows. Their resilience is a testament to human strength and a call for empathy and understanding. As their tapestry unfolds, we must adopt a nuanced approach, delicately weaving together their individual and collective pain threads. It is a call for healing, warmth, and the acknowledgment of their silenced cries and the embrace of their shattered dreams. And as the chapter closes, our hearts swell with sympathy for women like Akon, imprisoned not only by bars and walls but by the unspoken burdens they carry—a reflection of the profound struggles that women endure in the wake of war and calamity.

CHAPTER 14

EVIL OR ILLNESS

In communities overwhelmed by violence, a haunting question persists like a shadowy spectre: Why do certain individuals and communities act in ways that inflict harm, casting darkness on lives? Is it inherent malevolence, mental illness, or a psychological flaw? These questions haunt those who witness the aftermath of violence, struggling with the puzzle of human behaviour. Yet, in seeking answers, we often focus solely on the acts of violence, neglecting the complex roots intertwined with societal fabric that foster darkness.

Behind every act of violence are individuals and communities scarred by trauma, which disorients, silences, and distorts reality, leaving deep scars. This trauma fosters denial, blame-shifting, and collective amnesia as we evade the grim reality before us. To move towards healing and redemption, we must confront, acknowledge, and bear witness to the harrowing truths that have emerged. By standing together, embracing even the most horrifying details, we challenge our humanity. Ignoring, dismissing, or forgetting these truths makes us complicit in perpetuating inequality and inhumanity.

This chapter embarks on a journey through human behaviour's labyrinth, aiming to illuminate the shadows obscuring our understanding of violence. We delve into human psychology, exploring the collective trauma that affects both individuals and communities. Navigating this complex terrain, we brace ourselves for revelations that may challenge our core beliefs. This exploration demands us to question, empathize, and recognize the intricate beauty of the human experience.

Join me in confronting violence's enigma, challenging the notions of evil and illness, and exploring the interplay of factors that shape the human condition. In seeking understanding, let us find solace in healing's shared journey, with compassion and empathy guiding us through humanity's darkest aspects. As we search for answers, we must remember that profound revelations often emerge from complexity, transcending simplistic labels and exploring the human soul's myriad shades. Let's embark on this transformative odyssey together, deciphering the riddle at the heart of the human condition.

In 'Trauma and Recovery', Judith Herman writes:

> *"It is very tempting to take the side of the perpetrator. All the perpetrator asks is that the bystander do nothing. He appeals to the universal desire to see, hear, and speak no evil. The victim,*

on the contrary, asks the bystander to share the
burden of pain. The victim demands action,
engagement, and remembering".

Within the vast mosaic of human behaviour, a complex
interplay of elements shapes the trajectory of violence. While
trauma alone may not unlock the puzzle of violence and
self-destructive actions, it significantly impacts the South
Sudanese communities. Recognising violence's multifaceted
nature, we must not ignore trauma's profound influence on
behavioural patterns.

Structural discrimination, racial prejudices, and the spectre
of racism cast long shadows, embedding themselves within
systems and institutions and placing refugees, including the
South Sudanese, at a marked disadvantage. Their voyage to
new lands is shadowed by the remnants of war-torn origins,
a legacy that lingers within them. However, acknowledging
this surface awareness unveils a deeper truth—those escaping war-ravaged nations carry the scars of enduring conflict,
yet they persist with remarkable resilience. Embracing their
transition to new environments necessitates acknowledging
the critical role of trauma intervention and support for their
complete healing and purpose.

War's scars extend beyond the physical, deeply incising the
human psyche with pain and sorrow. The South Sudanese
carry the trauma of conflict and loss, a burden unimaginable
to many. In these moments of intense vulnerability, violence's
seeds find fertile ground. Trauma-influenced behaviours

become mechanisms to confront past horrors, sometimes bewildering onlookers.

In exploring human suffering, we must avoid simplifying the narrative to mere tales of evil or illness. Instead, we encounter a symphony of stories—individuals burdened with a collective history, seeking healing and redemption. The path to recovery meanders through trauma's maze, calling for our deepest compassion and understanding. It invites us to knit together cultural empathy's threads, recognising that war's wounds cross boundaries and initiate a united journey towards resilience.

Let us courageously face the complex reality that unfolds. Guided by empathy and illuminated by compassion, we delve into the human soul's depths. Together, we acknowledge the struggles and achievements, finding comfort in our common humanity. In demystifying violence, we uncover that true healing lies beyond judgment or condemnation, or the confines of prison—although these have their places—but in embracing our collective fragility. As we proceed, may we remain open to the transformative potential of shared responsibility and actions, crafting an understanding that transcends boundaries and unites us as a global family.

Two perspectives scrutinise the South Sudanese men, women, and youth, survivors of profound adversity from an early age. One perspective traces violence back to its roots—early suffering that catalyses a cycle of revenge-fuelled behaviours. Within pain and adversity's crucible, the seeds of aggression germinate, nourished by wounded souls' tears.

These individuals, robbed of innocence amidst turmoil, align with violence in a quest for honour and retribution, aiming to reclaim what was unjustly seized from them.

Yet, this path of aggression, with its deceptive allure, fails to deliver the resolution they yearn for—the seething shame and humiliation remain nestled deep within their hearts, untouched by each act of vengeance. A relentless cycle ensnares them, an intricate dance of violence and pain, where momentary honour reclaimed transforms into relentless bondage to aggression. Like a ravenous beast, their thirst for vindication knows no bounds, pushing them to seek new shores of justification, never realising that true healing eludes their grasp. Each act of violence chips away at the threshold for the next, desensitising the perpetrator to the gravity of their actions. Society's taboos against aggression become mere whispers in the wind, drowned out by the tempest of anger and revenge. They spiral further into the depths of their own creation, imprisoned by the very chains of violence they forged. The pursuit of aggression becomes an intoxicating solution, an addiction that offers momentary relief but tragically fails to mend the profound wounds of humiliation and dishonour.

As the darkness deepens, they find themselves lost in the labyrinth of their own making, yearning for escape yet unable to break free. The scars of their past pain merge with the fresh wounds they inflict, forming an indistinguishable tapestry of agony. They become prisoners of their own creation, trapped in the relentless grip of violent behaviour, forever haunted by the ghosts of their past, demons of their own doing, and an uncertain future.

In this unfolding tragedy, the quest for honour becomes a tragic irony, for the honour they seek is but a fleeting illusion, and the violence they wield only perpetuates the cycle of suffering. The path they tread leads not to redemption but to a perpetual cycle of self-inflicted wounds, a continuous battle with the shadows of their own souls. The roots of violence, deeply entrenched in the past, clutch at their hearts, refusing to release them from the chains of violence.

As we peer into the depths of this gloomy narrative, we are reminded of the human capacity for suffering and resilience. The path to healing lies not in perpetuating violence, but in recognising our shared humanity, sharing opportunities and resources, and embracing compassion. In the midst of this darkness, we must strive to find the light of understanding and empathy, for it is only through these virtues that we can break free from the relentless grip of violence and pave the way to a brighter future.

A second perspective emerges, challenging the notion that wrongdoing is an inexorable fate for those who have suffered unspeakable trauma. This philosophical and empirical view posits that the heart's sovereignty remains inviolable, endowed with the power of choice. It acts as a beacon of hope, illuminating the possibility of breaking free from the shackles of past afflictions and charting a different course—one guided by compassion and righteousness.

From this viewpoint, the human spirit stands as a fortress, capable of withstanding the onslaught of trauma and pain. Despite the unimaginable horrors they have endured, individuals retain the ability to choose a path that deviates from the treacherous road of malevolence. It is a testament to the indomitable strength of the human will, refusing to be consumed by the shadows cast upon their lives.

The choices made in the crucible of adversity possess profound power—they can shape the trajectory of tomorrow and forge a new narrative of healing and redemption. The path of righteousness may be arduous, fraught with challenges and doubts, but it remains a viable option—a beacon of light amid the encircling darkness. Within the heart of every individual lies the compass of conscience, guiding them away from the precipice of malevolence. Even amidst the chaos and turmoil, the flicker of goodness endures, a spark that can be nurtured into a roaring flame. Through wholesome systems of support and structures that foster healing instead of punishment, compassion, and empathy, individuals can take steps towards liberation from the cycle of violence and suffering. The human spirit is not a mere vessel tossed by the winds of fate; it is equipped with a rudder, allowing individuals to navigate the tumultuous waters of life. They can steer their destinies away from the treacherous currents of aggression and hatred, choosing instead the path of healing and reconciliation.

In this unfolding narrative, the triumph of the human spirit lies not in surrendering to the wounds of the past but in embracing the power of choice and the capacity for growth. With appropriate structures, systems, and support, each individual possesses the potential to transcend their past, to rise above the horrors they have endured, and to create a future that stands as a testament to their resilience.

As we delve deeper into this alternate perspective, we are reminded that the human experience is not confined to the boundaries of fate and circumstance. It is a symphony of choices, a tapestry of resilience, where the threads of compassion and strength interweave to create a masterpiece of healing and hope. In the face of darkness, this perspective reaffirms that the heart's sovereignty remains intact—a guiding light towards the path of righteousness. It is a call to embrace the power of choice, to eschew the allure of malevolence, and to journey towards a future where healing and redemption flourish like wildflowers after a storm.

In my own upbringing, a profound contrast emerges, revealing the divergent paths that can spring forth from shared hardships. In stark contrast, my path led me towards the refuge of non-violence, embarking on a lifelong quest to unravel the mysteries of violence itself. Despite the shared backdrop of a war-torn existence, our choices bore strikingly different fruits. This is evident within families, where some young people become heavily criminally involved while others pursue academic success, highlighting the divergent paths that can emerge from similar circumstances.

As I traverse the labyrinth of memories, I am compelled to abandon the notion that I was one who managed to "escape" the clutches of violence. The truth is that we all remain tethered to its haunting presence, forever enmeshed in its strands. Instead, I find myself seated on the other side of a narrow table, an observer who watches, listens, asks questions, and yearns to comprehend my people—those who reside on the spectrum where violence takes root in the human spirit. I am not set apart; rather, I am driven to contextualise, theorise, and expose the tangled web of collective traumas and the shadows of violence that loom over our lives.

When violence becomes a constant companion, its chilling presence weaves its way into the fabric of one's existence. It demands that we choose a side—a role to play within the narrative of affliction. We may find ourselves aligning with the perpetrators, the very architects of pain; or we may assume the roles of condemners, seeking justice for the tormented souls; or perhaps, like myself, we embark on the quest to comprehend the enigma of violence, its roots, and its tendrils that stretch far and wide. In the realm of violence and trauma, there are no easy answers or clean distinctions between right and wrong. It is a realm of complexity, where the human experience is shaped by the haunting echoes of suffering. The pathways we traverse are deeply intertwined with the collective narratives of our communities, etched with both sorrow and resilience.

In observing our parents' turbulent journey, I witness the turbulent undercurrents of suffering, forged from the tempestuous fires of the past. I recognise that some of their choices, like those of countless others, reflect a soul yearning for retribution, seeking to reclaim a semblance of honour lost in the tides of tragedy. For me, the path of non-violence offers solace—an attempt to heal the wounds of a war-torn past and to understand the depths of the human heart. Yet, even in my pursuit of understanding, I acknowledge that we all remain captives within the ring of violence, forever bound by its stark presence.

As I recount my own journey and that of my family and community members, I am reminded that within the folds of trauma and violence, there exists no clear escape, no easy resolution. Instead, we find ourselves entangled in the complexities of human experience, forever seeking to make sense of a world scarred by the indelible marks of suffering. Perhaps, the solutions lie as much with those in positions of power as with us. The structures that undermine the role of suffering, trauma, and resettlement in foreign lands may bear as much responsibility for our society's and people's healing as we do ourselves.

Within the unforgiving ring of violence and trauma, we find ourselves entangled, grappling with the weight of our choices and the collective burden we bear. No matter which side we align with—be it the perpetrators, the condemners, or the seekers of understanding—we remain enmeshed in the intricate dance between good and evil. It is a shared journey, woven deeply into the very fabric of our existence, where the pathway to redemption unfurls through the delicate threads of compassion and empathy. As we navigate the labyrinth of violence, we realise that its reach transcends borders, defying the boundaries of geography and culture. It is an all-encompassing force that touches lives across the globe, weaving its malevolent tapestry through the narratives of countless communities. Yet, amid the chaos and despair, there exists an unwavering beacon of hope—that of reclaiming our collective humanity.

The journey towards healing begins with the embrace of compassion—a recognition that we are all bound by the fragile thread of our shared humanity and responsibility to one another. In the midst of darkness, we must strive to see the flicker of light within each soul, understanding the pain and suffering that may have led them astray. Through empathy, we forge connections that traverse the chasms of differences, bridging the gaps that divide us. The dance of good and evil is a complex symphony that reverberates through the annals of history. Yet, even within the darkest notes, there lies the potential for redemption. It is the power of compassion that has the capacity to break the chains of violence, soften hardened hearts, and mend shattered souls. By extending our hand in empathy, we may not erase the scars of the past, but we can plant seeds of hope for a future adorned with unity and understanding.

In this journey towards healing, we discover that the boundaries dividing us are mere illusions. Beneath the surface, we are all connected by a universal yearning for peace, love, and acceptance. By recognising this shared struggle, we lay the foundation for a world where violence no longer prevails. As we navigate the labyrinth of violence and trauma, let us remember that we are all participants in this complex narrative. Together, by pooling our minds, expertise, and resources, we possess the power to break free from the cycle of aggression, to rise above violent currents, and to chart a course towards a society, communities, and families free from violence.

In the end, it is not merely about choosing a side within the ring of violence. Instead, it is a collective journey, where we walk hand in hand, acknowledging our shared struggles and striving to mend the fractures that divide us. In the embrace of compassion and empathy, we find the path towards healing—a path that leads us to the rediscovery of our collective humanity.

In the haunting realm of violent abuse, the psyche of individuals is not merely wounded; it is distorted, invaded, and even corrupted. The malevolence creeps into the victims' unconscious, weaving its dark threads through their essence. As they find themselves trapped in a world that rewards evil, the resources to resist its alluring call grow scarce.

These harrowing revelations give rise to profound questions that echo through the chambers of our conscience. Does the person whose psyche bears the scars of abuse become akin to one afflicted by an illness, a soul deserving of society's sympathy and understanding? Or does the corruption of their psyche, born from the malevolence they endured, render them predisposed to becoming morally tainted, robbed of the innocence they once held? If the latter is true, should we bestow our sympathy and resources upon them, acknowledging that the seeds of corruption were sown externally, imposed upon them from the shadows? Or should we hold them accountable like any other who commits evil deeds, for ultimately, they have become bearers of malice, not merely individuals with damaged psyches? And in this complex interplay of evil and innocence, where do the people of South Sudan find their place?

The distinction between evil and sickness blurs, as the crimes against humanity reveal their dual nature. The malevolence signifies a moral failing, while the sickness embodies the distortion in the labyrinth of their minds, intensifying the evil that sprouts forth. Foot soldiers, mere pawns in the vicious game of so-called judicial executions in South Sudan, succumb to the allure of evil regimes, becoming conduits of darkness. We are tempted to hold them morally responsible for the horrors they unleash, as their choices defy the very essence of their consciousness. Yet, in the shadows of their actions, some may call out for our sympathy. Amidst the ravages of war, the trauma they endure, and the misguided leadership that steers them astray, they lack the guiding models to lead them away from the path of violence.

Within these troubled waters, Richard Rhodes (2015) paints a chilling canvas of the interplay between violence and brutality. Criminal violence, he suggests, finds its origins in the brutal experiences imposed upon vulnerable children, who later return to society as vengeful agents of wrath. But as Rhodes (2015) prompts us to consider, if violence is indeed a choice they make, and thus their personal responsibility, then our failure to protect them from such harrowing choices becomes a choice of our own.

As we grapple with these tangled webs of evil, sickness, and responsibility, we must also confront our role in shaping the fates of those who traverse the treacherous path of malevolence. Within the hearts of those affected by violence, the struggle to distinguish between culpability and compassion emerges as a moral imperative, one that has the power to shape the course of humanity's destiny.

CHAPTER 15

"DEAD BUT NOT BURIED": PSYCHOLOGICAL STRUGGLES OF SOUTH SUDANESE WAR VETERANS

"Before, he was good. But then he went to war and saw many people die, and although he survived, he became abnormal. He is always angry at everyone and every little thing and does not like someone talking nearby. He quarrels with me and with other people, not like before. Sometime at night he cries to God that he is dying. His suffering is increasing by day. The suffering is just too much, he is dead but not buried."

- The Wife of a Veteran

A Kenyan psychologist Benjamine Zulu once said, "*A person can die at age 26 and live on until they are buried at 75*," meaning that there are those among us who have experienced so much suffering that they have died mentally and emotionally but still breathe until they reach old age. In the labyrinth of war-torn souls, we find the haunting tale of those who bear the weight of death without the respite of burial. This is not a metaphor born of poetic fancy but a stark truth that reverberates through the testimonies of South Sudanese veterans and their families. These men, once noble and good, have been scarred by the harrowing spectacles of war. The echoes of countless lives lost have etched an indelible mark on their spirits, transforming them into aberrations of their former selves. A desolate landscape now pervades their hearts, where anger simmers like molten lava, and the simplest of human interactions spark an inferno of emotions.

In the hushed corners of the night, their souls cry out to the heavens, pleading for respite from the agony that refuses to subside. The suffering, relentless and unyielding, chokes their very essence, leaving them haunted by ghosts of the past. They are the walking wounded, existing in a limbo between life and death, for though their bodies breathe, their spirits languish in emotional, psychological, and spiritual desolation.

The wives of these veterans, once familiar with their loving husbands, now bear witness to the metamorphosis. They recount tales of men who have become strangers to themselves and those around them. The war has robbed them of the essence of humanity, leaving in its wake an abyss of rage and despondency. The weight of trauma has rendered them emotionally numb, unable to feel even the gentlest stirrings of compassion or affection.

This malady runs deep within their souls, causing a profound detachment from their own humanity. For some, the guilt of taking lives weighs like an impenetrable shroud, yet remorse remains a foreign emotion, held captive by the horrors of war. They speak of atrocities committed without a flicker of remorse, for they were trapped in a cycle where survival mandated acts of violence. The rules of war, if ever they existed, demanded that they kill or be killed, and thus, their conscience became a casualty of this brutal calculus.

These tales of emotional death and spiritual decay are not confined to the realm of metaphor. They embody the essence of trauma that transcends mere corporeal existence. These men have witnessed the darkest abyss of humanity and emerged hollow, bereft of the very essence that once defined them. In the vortex of pain and suffering, they have become the living dead.

To truly understand this condition, we must delve into the annals of South Sudanese history, where the roots of trauma stretch back to the days of colonisation. Civil wars, famine, displacement, and the desperate search for asylum in foreign lands have etched scars upon their collective psyche. Before the violent spectre of colonialism, their society had its own harmonious family and community structures. In this patri-archal domain, roles were well-defined, weaving a tapestry of interconnected lives. The man, woman, and children each held their place in the intricate web of society.

Yet, the ravages of war and displacement disrupted this delicate balance, ushering in a torrent of family dysfunction, disintegration, and an alarming surge in criminality and self-destructive behaviours. These men, adrift and lost, grapple with feelings of hopelessness and worthlessness. The very fabric of society has unravelled, leaving them with an overwhelming sense of displacement, even in their own homes and communities.

The wounds run deep, etched by the passage of time and generations of suffering. It is not merely the physical scars that bear witness to their pain, but the indomitable spirit that struggles to find meaning amidst the ruins. To unravel the torment of those who are dead but not buried, we must navigate the labyrinth of history and, in doing so, strive to heal the wounds that hold these men hostage to their own anguish. Only through understanding and empathy can we hope to breathe life back into their spirits, guiding them towards the elusive light of redemption and peace.

In the echoes of Chinua Achebe's poignant words, "When the centre can no longer hold, things fall apart," we find a haunting reflection of the disintegration that befalls South Sudanese families. Rooted in a patriarchal society, where men once stood as pillars—providing, protecting, and guiding their families—they now face a cruel fate where war and hardship have stripped them of their roles. The wounds they bear, both physical and emotional, are profound, and as they seek refuge in foreign lands, the burden of settlement challenges compounds their suffering.

In the diaspora, these men find themselves grappling with a profound loss of identity, their very essence shattered by the trauma they endured. The roles that once defined them as the centre of their families have been usurped, leaving them adrift and hopeless in their struggle to find purpose. It is in this dark abyss of trauma that they begin to fall apart, and the ripple effect of their disintegration reverberates through the entire family.

Before migration, these men held the delicate threads that wove the family fabric together, providing stability and guidance. Now, that pivotal role is vacated, leaving the family without its compass. Women and authorities step in to fill the void, but they cannot replace the unique presence of these men. The interplay of trauma and hopelessness weaves a vicious cycle, eroding the very foundations of family unity.

As we examine the lives of these men, we bear witness to the profound consequences of their suffering on the younger generations. The children, once witnesses to their fathers as protectors and providers, now observe a world fractured by violence and loss. What they witness at a young age shapes their perception of what is acceptable and what is not, influencing their understanding of how men should treat women and those around them.

When society intervenes to "save" women and children from these "violent men," the cycle of violence is inadvertently perpetuated. By removing these men without addressing the root causes of their suffering, we perpetuate a legacy of trauma that passes from one generation to the next. The intergenerational transmission of trauma leaves an indelible mark on the minds and hearts of the youth, perpetuating a cycle of violence and disintegration.

To break this cycle, we must take a closer look at the lives of these men and offer comprehensive support that addresses the roots of their trauma. Providing avenues for healing and empowerment can restore their sense of purpose and reintegrate them as vital members of their families and communities. Only then can we begin to mend the ruptured bonds and rebuild the centre that holds families together.

In the quest to heal these fractured souls, we must embrace empathy and understanding, recognising the profound impact of war and displacement on their lives. It is only through healing the wounded hearts of these men that we can break the chains of violence and create a legacy of resilience and unity for future generations. Let us not forsake the fallen centre, for in its restoration lies the hope for a brighter and more harmonious future for South Sudanese families and their communities.

In the dim light of a New Year's Eve, I found myself immersed in the heart-wrenching scenes of two mothers seeking refuge at a family violence centre where I was doing a night shift, each carrying their own burdens of trauma and desperation. Intoxicated by the numbing embrace of substances, they stumbled back into the refuge with their children in tow, bearing the weight of their broken lives. One of the mothers, less intoxicated, managed to take her children upstairs, seeking solace in slumber amidst the chaos. The other, engulfed in the haze of her inebriation, clung to the semblance of normalcy by attempting to have dinner. Yet, the heartache was palpable as her two boys, just seven and eight years old, withered in exhaustion and hunger, their young faces bearing the marks of suffering endured under the scorching sun of a 34-degree heat.

As one of the boys, his parched throat yearning for water, repeatedly asked for a drink, his mother's promises of action remained hollow, lost in the oblivion of her intoxication. Unable to bear the sight of the child's suffering, I rose to offer help, only to be met with a tumultuous outburst of anger. The echoes of her shattered voice reverberated through the room, painting a picture of a mother drowning in her own pain. Yet, amidst this heartbreaking scene, a beacon of innocence and wisdom emerged in the form of a seven-year-old boy. He approached with eyes that spoke of both sadness and exhaustion, a burden too heavy for his tender shoulders. With courage that belied his age, he offered solace to a stranger, understanding the depth of his mother's pain.

As the boy expressed his belief that his mother would be better in the morning, his words pierced the tumultuous air, reaching deep into my heart. Tears streamed down my face, my emotions laid bare by the weight of the moment. I knelt down to match the boy's height, gently reassuring him that he and his brother were safe, enveloping him in a cocoon of love and hope. Yet, just as one heartache unfolded, another awaited at the doorstep of a friend in need. Visiting a friend, a mother abandoned by her husband and left to fend for herself and her two children, the stark reality of their situation struck me like a sudden gust of wind. The cupboards were bare, and the atmosphere was fraught with tension.

In the midst of a conversation that quickly escalated, the mother's frustration reached a boiling point, and violence erupted. The young children bore the brunt of her pain, leaving me paralysed with rage and grief. In a desperate attempt to shield the innocent, I intervened, vowing to take the children under my wing if the violence did not cease. Amidst the turmoil, an internal storm of emotions raged within me, torn between compassion and anger. As groceries were ordered and prepared, silence enveloped the room, granting space for reflection. The children slumbered, their peaceful innocence a stark contrast to the turbulent emotions swirling around them.

In the stillness, a conversation between the mother and me began, a dialogue that sought to bridge the chasm of pain and despair. Unspoken apologies and understanding took root, both souls burdened by the weight of their suffering, seeking solace and connection. In the wake of these heart-wrenching encounters, I was left to grapple with the haunting realisation of the cycle of violence and trauma. The innocent children, caught in the crossfire of pain and desperation, were at risk of inheriting a legacy of dysfunction and abuse.

A profound desire to break this cycle of suffering stirred within me, pushing me to extend a lifeline of compassion and support. Yet, the path ahead was fraught with challenges, uncertainties, and the unknown future. In the depths of despair, a glimmer of hope emerged. The observer recognised that the healing journey would not be easy, but the power of understanding and collective intervention holds the potential to mend shattered lives and lead the way towards a brighter tomorrow.

The shattering breakdown of relationships through family violence can only be likened to the horrors of war, trauma, social inequalities, gender, cultural structures, and systems of oppression. Like soldiers returning from the frontlines, scarred and broken, the casualties of domestic strife extend beyond the direct combatants. In this tumultuous battleground, the innocent children emerge as the invisible casualties, robbed of their fundamental right to live peacefully and freely as carefree souls.

These young ones grow up amidst the chaos, their tender minds moulded by dysfunction and violence. The only language they come to know for expressing emotions is one of anger, emotional withdrawal, or manipulation. Lost and confused, they carry a burden far beyond their years, disguised by the veneer of tough exteriors, shielding their wounded hearts.

In addressing those who perpetrate violence, some may argue that it's an excuse to avoid accountability or punishment. However, the truth lies deeper. The adage "hurt people hurt people" reveals the sad reality that those who inflict pain upon others are often themselves carrying the weight of their own scars. The cycle of hurting becomes a never-ending loop, passing pain from one wounded soul to another.

To address these individuals, it is essential to delve into the root causes of their behaviour. This exploration is not an excuse to overlook the pain they've inflicted or the damage they've wrought upon victims, but rather an attempt to provide interventions and preventive measures that yield lasting positive impact.

Violence in our community transcends simplistic explanations of instinctive male nature or inherent evilness. Instead, it finds its origins in traumatic experiences, racism, discrimination, marginalisation, shame, and the lingering guilt of being treated as less than human, as mere shadows in society's eyes. To dismantle the webs of abuse and violence, we must confront these intersecting challenges and barriers head-on. The key lies in healing and providing resources to empower individuals, allowing them to reclaim their humanity and feel a sense of equality in a world that has often treated them unjustly.

Even in the face of seemingly senseless and incomprehensible violent behaviour, I am convinced that there exists an underlying set of conditions, a chain of irrational, self-destructive, and unconscious motives. With dedicated study and understanding, these motives can be unravelled and potentially resolved, offering a glimmer of hope for a path towards healing and peace. The journey may be arduous, but every step taken in pursuit of a violence-free world is a step closer to redemption and transformation.

CHAPTER 16

REPAIR

We might not reach a point in life whereby our bodies will longer keep the scores as Dr. Bessel van der Kolk famous book "*The Body Keeps The Score*" explains. Therefore, in facing the profound challenges posed by traumatic events and conflicts and their devastating consequences, we are compelled to ask: How can we foster healing and transformation? How can we reduce the perpetration of violence and rates of recidivism within our society, especially among communities with deeply wounded backgrounds, such as refugees? How can we, as individuals and as a society, work towards restoring awareness of our interconnection and breaking free from the cycles of violence and suffering? How can we ensure that violence is addressed across all aspects of human lives? What does repair looks and what will it take to make this work tangible and sustainable? All these important questions become a part of our reparative quest in today's society and going forth. Informed by research, personal experiences, and observations of communities from refugee backgrounds, as well as an awareness of our past and current systemic structures, the answer lies in multifaceted approaches that address human health (both physical and psychological), class, race, gender, socioeconomic status, age, criminality, and a social justice approaches.

First and foremost, we must recognise that the reduction, flattening, and separation from perceived enemies are rooted in fear and survival instincts, often amplified by the mechanisms of shock and adrenaline. To understand the underlying causes and address them effectively, we need to acknowledge that perpetuating war against perceived enemies is not a sustainable solution. Instead, we must strive to build bridges of understanding and empathy, recognising the humanity in each individual, irrespective of their differences.

One of the crucial steps in this process is to challenge the notion of making enemies larger than life. By cultivating a culture of compassion and open dialogue, we can dismantle the barriers that lead to mass dissociation and disembodiment. We must confront the plight of frightened refugees and vulnerable immigrant children, seeking humane and just solutions that protect their dignity and well-being. Additionally, we must address the 'mental suitcases' filled with fragments and ghosts that people carry within themselves. Encouraging open conversations about trauma and fostering a supportive environment can allow individuals to confront and integrate these dissociated aspects, paving the way for healing and the restoration of our multidimensional selves.

Education and awareness play crucial roles in breaking the cycle of violence and trauma. By fostering understanding and empathy from an early age, we can instil in future generations the values of the interconnectedness of human lives, regardless of race, gender, class, age, or sexual orientation. This entails promoting social and emotional learning, cultivating conflict resolution skills, and encouraging peaceful dialogue.

Furthermore, it is imperative to acknowledge the profound impact of social and economic inequality in perpetuating violence and shame within our society. As we aspire to create a more just and inclusive world, we must dismantle systems that perpetuate division and degradation based on socio-economic status, race, or gender. Our pursuit of equality begins with our political leaders, who must champion policies that uplift and empower marginalized communities.

But it does not end there. The quest for a more compassionate and equitable society extends to all realms of our institutions, including our judicial system, law enforcement agencies, and healthcare providers. To effect real change, we need a comprehensive approach that goes beyond mere token gestures of cultural competency training. Instead, we must embed an understanding of the unique health challenges faced by different communities, especially refugee communities, within our healthcare system. Equipping health practitioners with the necessary resources and expertise to address these specific needs is paramount.

Within the criminal justice system, prioritising the mental well-being of law enforcement officers is imperative. These individuals often encounter trauma in their duties, and supporting their mental health is crucial for ensuring they respond with compassion and understanding to victims of violence. Enhancing relations between the police and the general public is key to building trust and fostering respect throughout the criminal investigation process, ensuring justice begins from the moment officers arrive at the crime scene and continues to the final judgment.

Regrettably, the experiences of the heavily policed South Sudanese community and other Black communities in Australia highlight a significant disparity in the treatment they receive. A paradigm shift is urgently required to move from a military approach to a more empathetic and community-centred policing philosophy.

Addressing socioeconomic conditions beyond law enforcement and healthcare is essential for lasting change. Providing opportunities for sustainable employment enables individuals to support themselves and their families, alleviating the reliance on social welfare. Everyone deserves the chance to thrive, irrespective of their background or circumstances.

In our efforts to welcome and support refugees, the importance of trauma-informed settlement services cannot be overstated. The journey for refugees encompasses not just physical relocation but also emotional and psychological healing. By incorporating trauma-informed approaches into settlement services, we can more effectively address the pre-migration traumas refugees bring with them, facilitating a more compre-hensive and compassionate settlement process.

Tackling these root causes of violence and shame is key to creating a truly inclusive, empathetic, and resilient society. This is a collective endeavour that requires dedication and unity from all community sectors. As we progress towards this vision, we become the conductors of empathy, guiding humanity's orchestra towards a harmonious and compassion-ate symphony. The journey may be fraught with challenges, but the destination offers a world where violence is replaced by peace, shame by understanding, and healing becomes our collective anthem. Let us walk this path together, hand in hand, towards this transformative future.

In our quest for healing and integration, investing in mental health support and trauma-informed care is crucial. Making resources for healing and counselling accessible can facilitate the restoration of embodiment and the tapping into deeper resilience. Additionally, considering the broader social context is vital in the healing journey. Equal distribution of resources and efforts to mitigate class disparities can foster a more supportive and nurturing environment for healing. Since trauma often amplifies social inequalities, addressing these disparities is critical for a holistic healing process. Liberating ourselves from the chains of trauma necessitates a collective endeavour to create a compassionate and supportive commu-nity that promotes self-exploration.

The path towards healing and transformation, albeit fraught with challenges, holds promise. By acknowledging our interconnectedness, recognising the pervasive impact of trauma, and cultivating empathy and understanding, we can work towards a more compassionate and peaceful world. It is this collective action and dedication to healing that paves the way for a future where violence and suffering yield to unity, love, and a profound sense of shared humanity.

Trauma work is indeed a deep and transformative journey, resembling a spiritual quest for recovery. It entails delving into our essence to unearth the dormant "ghosts" within us, those fragments of our dissociated selves buried in the icy confines of our psyche. These ghosts represent the fragmented parts of our identity, the unacknowledged traumas, and the wounds that still shape our responses and behaviours under stress.

The aim of trauma work is not to perpetually revisit every painful memory but to revive, liberate, and reintegrate these lost parts of ourselves into our body and being. This reintegration process is essential for reconnecting with our core self and unlocking deeper resilience and higher capabilities. Similarly, just as individuals are inherently designed to grow and evolve, so too are collectives, races, cultures, and nations. When collective traumas obstruct our shared progress and understanding, the collective body must address its own "ghosts". Parts of the collective may become detached, refusing to acknowledge shared wounds, yet every aspect is vital for the overall health of the community.

To begin the process of healing and restoring our collective shadows, we must advance beyond strategies that solely recognize reactive violence and seek punishment without delving into the origins of such behaviours. Collective trauma work necessitates mutual presence and communal witness as we unite to acknowledge and heal the wounds afflicting us as a collective. Ignoring and suppressing our collective shadows will only continue the haunting cycle, transmitting unresolved trauma from one generation to the next, thereby affecting our children and their descendants in a perpetual cycle of karma and drama.

Embarking on trauma work, both individually and collectively, allows us to escape these repetitive patterns. Through healing and integration, we can forge a new path marked by mutual understanding, empathy, and collective peace. By bringing the ghosts of our past into the light of consciousness, we free ourselves from the chains of trauma and lay the foundations for a future rooted in healing, growth, and unity.

In our endeavour to heal our collective wounds, we seize the opportunity to break the cycles of violence and suffering that have plagued us for too long. With compassion, presence, and a commitment to inner and collective transformation, we embark on a journey of profound healing, reclaiming our wholeness and moulding a future unburdened by past afflictions. As we unite in this shared endeavour, we sow the seeds of hope, love, and collective liberation for future generations.

Healing trauma and its repercussions are deeply entrenched in human relationships and connections. Although therapeutic methods like the neurosequential model and talk therapy show promise in addressing trauma, the deepest healing for those who have endured extreme violence, war, or abuse often occurs outside the confines of therapy. Solely punitive approaches fall short, as trauma healing demands a holistic and compassionate strategy.

Trauma's impact on human relationships is undeniable. Be it the aftermath of war, natural disasters, or repeated abuse, the most harrowing outcome is the breakdown of human connections. For those from backgrounds of war and extreme violence, the rupture of relational ties can be particularly profound. As social creatures, our greatest tragedies stem from the loss of significant relationships.

Recovery from trauma and neglect is intrinsically linked to the restoration of trust, the revival of confidence, and reconnection with love and security. While medication and therapy offer valuable support in symptom management and emotional processing, genuine healing and recovery hinge on enduring, caring relationships with others, including decision-makers in our lives. Through these bonds, individuals rediscover a sense of safety, understanding, and belonging.

In therapy, the relationship with the therapist is critical. This bond fosters trust, safety, and a readiness to address and heal from trauma. While therapeutic techniques are important, the essence of therapy resides in the therapeutic alliance and the empathetic support provided by the therapist. Healing from trauma requires a comprehensive approach that includes human connections, compassionate care, equitable resource access, and the nurturing support of the therapeutic relationship. Recognizing the importance of relationships in healing allows us to foster a more compassionate, understanding world that empowers trauma survivors to reclaim their lives.

Amidst the challenges faced, hope shines for the children and young individuals aiming to navigate away from the pitfalls of the criminal justice system. Their redemption lies not within the impersonal confines of institutions but in the supportive embrace of their community and loved ones. Families, friends, and esteemed figures provide a sanctuary, tolerant of their weaknesses and vulnerabilities, guiding them towards growth and opportunity, and laying the groundwork for their futures. In their quest for a safe and peaceful haven, they seek a social fabric that offers reassurance and a sense of belonging, enveloped in the warmth of love. This nurturing social environment is what their spirits most deeply yearn for—to heal the scars of their past.

This longing is not limited to individuals but resonates throughout the traumatized community and nation as a collective call for healing. A chorus of hearts in search of restoration, yearning for a nurturing community to protect them from the anguish, distress, and loss stemming from past traumas. In this healing journey, a transformative magic occurs—any contribution towards healing, care, and relationships becomes key to mending their broken spirits.

For those tormented souls, what resonates with echoes of hope is consistent, patient, and repetitive loving care. A symphony of compassion orchestrates their path towards rejuvenation, like a gentle stream slowly mending the fractured banks of their emotions. However, we must be wary of the pitfalls in the recovery path. A well-intentioned but inadequately trained cadre of so-called Western mental health "professionals" must not hastily invade their inner sanctums post-trauma, or coerce them and their communities to unveil their anguish.

Regrettably, this highlights a paradox—the most vulnerable to trauma's claws often lack a nurturing, supportive family and community. This cruel irony makes it daunting to deliver effective aid through existing systems. The battle is tough, for it is within the cradle of healthy communities that seeds of inter-personal traumatic events are often pre-emptively addressed. Yet, as our society becomes increasingly mobile, the delicate threads of social connection fray, exposing everyone to vulner-ability's harsh winds.

Therefore, the solution lies not in solitary remedies or quick fixes but in a tapestry woven by many hands. It is a collective endeavour to build resilient communities and mend frac-tured hearts. In fostering a haven of solace and compassion, we nurture healing roots that extend beyond the immediate, healing past wounds and sowing hope for future generations.

One of humanity's most marvellous traits is our ability to learn and evolve. Our memories, enriched by Western tech-nological marvels, allow us to benefit from our predecessors' wisdom. Yet, a subtle irony persists—the technologies designed to unite us often drive us apart, disrupting and sometimes forsaking the extended family, a cornerstone of human social life.

The breakdown of the nuclear family garners much atten-tion, yet the dissolution of the extended family remains a quieter concern. I firmly believe that preserving the nuclear family requires elevating the extended family's importance. As technology advances, we drift further from our evolutionary environments, often neglecting our basic human needs and veering towards harmful paths.

Ironically, Western psychology, through the "self-care" movement on social media, has contributed to this trend of detachment. For too long, mental health professionals propagated the idea that psychological health could be achieved without social support. The fallacy that one can only love oneself and that relationships are unnecessary contradicted our biology—we thrive on deep, interdependent human contact.

Remember the civil war times, when families, ravaged by violence, found solace in neighbours' embrace, who took in orphaned children despite their scarcity. This truth resounds with clarity: self-love sprouts from being loved and continually experiencing love, nurtured by genuine human connections.

As we navigate progress, let's not abandon the invaluable bonds of our extended families. In an era where technology lures us into virtual realms, may we remember the power of real, face-to-face interactions. Just as our ancestors built strong communal ties, we too should cherish the bonds that unite us as a human family.

In history's reverberating echoes, we must heed our biology's wisdom. We are destined to thrive not in isolation but embraced by loving kinship, within both nuclear and extended families, enriching our spirits and fostering resilience that spans generations. It's time to revive the 'village' concept in raising children.

Amidst history's shifting tides, an undeniable truth emerges: the capacity to love blooms in human connection's embrace. As societies awaken to the realization that vital mental health components have been overlooked in modernity's rush, we face distressing evidence—the rise in depression rates within our communities. Parents exist bodily but emotionally numb; young souls succumb to suicide's depths and the criminal justice system's grasp. The answer lies not solely in expanding justice centres like prisons or imposing harsher sentences but in a deeper, trauma-informed healing approach.

In the face of war trauma, family breakdowns, bullying, substance abuse, and settlement challenges faced by our youth, the need for a trauma-healing approach is starkly clear. The modern world's shallow substitutes push us further from mental well-being's sanctity.

With parents uneasy over the internet, media, drugs, predators, and economic disparities, our values in responding to these crises come into question. Despite varied viewpoints, the unhealthy nature of our current lifestyle is undeniable.

Now is the time for leaders, policymakers, law enforcement, service providers, and health practitioners to ask how we can heal and build our communities in this 'modern' world. A collective effort, grounded in compassion, understanding, and the pursuit of genuine connections, will guide us towards restoration and true well-being. It is our shared duty to weave a healing tapestry, rekindling the love that unites us as a resilient, united community.

Within troubled individuals lies a hidden realm of pain—a

cauldron of anguish stirring irritability, anxiety, and aggression. Yet, we must resist the temptation to view the traumatised solely through a lens of judgement, assuming they should "know better" and make more favourable choices. Punitive approaches, though seemingly attractive, prove futile in the face of profound suffering. Regrettably, our system fails to recognise this, favouring "quick fixes" that are ephemeral and result in extended punishments when they inevitably fall short.

Our call is for programmes and resources that understand the futility of punishment, deprivation, and force, as these only serve to re-traumatise individuals, deepening their plight. From the crucible of my own experiences, I have learned a poignant lesson—that the act of paying attention and listening can have transformative power. The mirroring neurobiology of our brains allows us to find calm and centre ourselves, opening the gateway to offering solace to others. Yet, our system seems to have lost sight of this wisdom, caught in a cycle of hasty reactions rather than thoughtful responses.

Prevention does not start at the moment of reaction; it is cultivated through meticulous study and understanding of underlying issues. Approaches carefully designed to address these concerns are key to genuine healing. Patience becomes our ally on this journey, for recovery is an intricate tapestry that requires time and unwavering dedication. The duration and intensity of trauma dictate the variety of approaches needed to restore equilibrium, necessitating honouring the uniqueness of each individual's healing process.

Empowering people to reclaim agency over their therapeutic

interactions becomes the cornerstone of recovery. Trauma, fundamentally, heralds a profound sense of powerlessness and loss of control; our therapeutic efforts must acknowledge this reality. Coercive methods, forceful and demanding, only plant seeds of fear that hinder progress. Safety, the sanctuary of recovery, must be cherished and nurtured above all.

Trauma's sinister tendrils often intertwine with other mental health problems, breeding behavioural issues and feeding the cycle of violence that plagues our community. Regrettably, the very systems meant to aid are tainted by coercive practices, further exacerbating the troubles they seek to remedy. To effect change, we must educate professionals across all sectors, imparting the profound truths about trauma and its impact. The justice system, child protection, and mental health care must align with this understanding, seeking approaches that reduce harm and heal.

Our endeavour cannot evade the grand political debates of our time—globalisation, the spectre of "wars", and economic inequality. To unravel trauma's web, we must face these challenges with courage and determination, dismantling the barriers that stand between healing and those in need.

I humbly acknowledge that I do not possess all the answers. Yet, I find solace in the belief that we are not solitary beings but rather a social species, intricately woven with mind, body, and soul. Within us reside unique capacities and vulnerabilities, while our brains, like skilled artisans, mould themselves through practice. Armed with this understanding, we can dare to pose the right questions, and in doing so, unlock the secrets that lead to healing and wholeness.

The journey of healing begins with the recognition that untransformed trauma has a dangerous tendency to transfer its wounds to others. But it is within our power to break this chain of suffering, transforming transferred trauma into a force of renewal and restoration. This metamorphosis requires not only a collective willingness to heal but also an unwavering commitment to support healing initiatives, approaches, and programmes. Resources must be allocated wisely, directed towards the cultivation of mental, physical, and spiritual well-being.

As we embark on this profound mission, let us remember that every individual, every community, carries the potential to create a ripple of positive change that reverberates through generations. It begins with healing ourselves, tending to the deep wounds within our souls, and finding solace in our interconnectedness. For in this shared tapestry of life, we find the threads of compassion, empathy, and love that weave us into a compassionate, self-reliant, and violence-free community.

Let us extend a hand of understanding to those who bear the weight of trauma, cherishing them as they embark on their journey of healing. Together, we can forge a new path, guided by the principles of respect, tolerance, and empathy. As we stand united, we shall weather the storms of adversity, transforming challenges into stepping stones towards a brighter future.

In the tapestry of our lives, every thread is vital, every voice essential. Let us stand together, shoulder to shoulder, embracing the complexity of human existence, forging a symphony of harmony and hope. May we never forget that the power to heal resides within each one of us, and it is through our collective efforts that we shall build a sanctuary of compassion and care.

The road ahead may be arduous, but our spirits soar with the belief that a healed and harmonious world is within reach. It is time to rise as a united force, champions of transformation, catalysts of change. Let us leave no stone unturned, no heart untouched by the healing grace.

In the embrace of empathy, we shall vanquish the darkness of trauma, replacing it with the radiance of resilience and renewal. As the dawn of a new era breaks, let us walk together, step by step, forging a future brimming with love, peace, and understanding. Together, let us create a world where trauma is but a distant memory, and love reigns supreme. For this is the legacy we leave for generations to come—a testament to the indomitable spirit of humanity.

Education also plays a crucial role in this transformational process. By teaching the value of non-violence, conflict resolution, and empathy from a young age, we can instil these principles as essential components of our societal fabric. Empowering the next generation with the tools to navigate conflicts peacefully will pave the way for a more harmonious and just world.

Healing and reconciliation are not simple or linear processes, but they are essential for the well-being of individuals and societies alike. It requires a willingness to confront the painful past and listen to the voices of those silenced by violence. With political, social, criminal justice, and economic approaches that acknowledge individuals' backgrounds and their needs to thrive in their communities and individual lives, we can begin the journey of healing. By acknowledging the trauma and pain, we start to reclaim lost dignity and find a path towards communal and self-actualisation.

CHAPTER 17

TRAUMA-INFORMED PRACTICE

Traditionally, we associate trauma-informed care with health-care and clinical psychology. But in recent years, experts like Bessel van der Kolk, Judith Herman, and Gabor Mate have shown its value extends beyond these fields. This approach is increasingly recommended for various professions, especially for individuals dealing with past or ongoing trauma.

Interestingly, the criminal justice system, which has historically focused on punitive measures, is starting to see the benefits of this approach. It's becoming clear that a trauma-informed perspective is crucial across all sectors. As society deals with ongoing issues of violence and trauma, both at home and internationally, adopting a trauma-informed mindset is more vital than ever.

Violence and Trauma in Our Communities

The exposure to violence, whether directly in the myth of wars against nations, national civil wars, through media, or social platforms, has become disturbingly common. This not only impacts individual mental health but also fuels further violence. Recent violent acts, from street crimes to mass attacks, underscore the need for understanding and addressing the underlying and the ongoing trauma.

Just as much as individuals within communities, professionals studying or working in violent environments are themselves at risk of vicarious trauma. This includes scholars, law enforcement, and healthcare workers, particularly in areas like Australia and against the backdrop of global conflicts such as in Ukraine and Sudan. As a scholar focusing on violence and trauma, I am deeply concerned about the transgenerational impact of trauma. This ongoing cycle threatens youth mental health and could lead to an increase in future violent behaviours.

Beyond Punishment:
Understanding and Healing

Recognising violence as both a trigger and a response to trauma helps us look beyond simple punitive measures. We need to explore the deep-seated historical roots of violence and its ongoing impact on society. By understanding these patterns, we can start to see acts of dysfunction as expressions of unresolved trauma passed down through generations.

This understanding shifts our perspective and encourages us to think about creating a society that is not just less violent but is actively caring, inclusive, nurturing, and supportive. However, with the rise of authoritarian politics and widespread disillusionment with traditional politics, envisioning a trauma-free society becomes challenging but not impossible.

The Role of Trauma in Shaping Future Perspectives

Research indicates that trauma can impair an individual's ability to think about the future. Neurobiological studies, including those using functional Magnetic Resonance Imaging, show that the same brain regions process past and future thinking. Unresolved trauma can thus limit our ability to envision and strive for a better future.

Evidence supports holistic trauma healing interventions that incorporate comprehensive mental health and psychosocial support. These approaches can reduce societal violence and enhance our capacity in five key areas: belief in our ability to effect change, understanding complex systems, perceiving time effectively, caring for others, and being open to different possibilities. This groundwork helps equip current and future generations to identify new ways to foster community well-being.

Understanding trauma's role in current levels of violence is crucial for creating conditions for a society that can move beyond endless cycles of violence and trauma. A trauma-informed approach isn't just beneficial; it's necessary for building a healthier, more resilient, and possibly less violent society.

What Does Trauma-Informed Practice Look Like?

Therapeutic Approach

In a trauma-informed therapeutic setting, the ethos is centred around creating a safe and supportive environment. This approach is skilfully encapsulated by the principle, *"Do no harm,"* which guides practitioners to engage without judgment, fostering a sense of safety that builds trust. Here, every interaction is an opportunity to affirm, educate, and empathise with the person seeking help, always treating them with the utmost dignity and respect.

This method involves a holistic engagement, supporting individuals to heal from past harms and preventing future ones. It prioritises resilience and personal agency, focusing on recovery, finding deeper meaning in experiences, recognising potential triggers, restoring the power of choice, and maintaining overall safety and well-being. As Maya Angelou once said, "I can be changed by what happens to me, but I refuse to be reduced by it." This sentiment is at the heart of the therapeutic approach, empowering individuals to rise above their circumstances.

Trauma-Informed Practice

Trauma-informed practice recognises that trauma is wide-spread, affecting both those who receive and those who provide services. It is more than a method; it's a shift in perspective that sees the 'whole person' rather than a single aspect of their experience. As Judith Herman rightly noted, "The survivor's need is not just to confront or re-live the trauma...but to become the principal author of her own life story." This practice supports this journey, being holistic, Empowering, and focusing on the strengths of each individual.

This approach is collaborative and reflective, ensuring that it adapts and responds to the needs of those involved. It aims to provide a safe space that covers physical, emotional, spiritual, and cultural aspects, thereby promoting a comprehensive sense of safety. In doing so, trauma-informed practice creates an environment where healing is not just possible but is actively facilitated, supporting individuals in reclaiming their lives and narratives.

Core Trauma-Informed Principles

Safety

Safety is a cornerstone of trauma-informed practice, covering both emotional and physical dimensions. As discussed in the chapters above, people and communities escaping war zones such as the South Sudanese in Australia may have escaped the physical threat to by migrating to Australia but because of structural, economic, social class, and cultural differences, they often than not feel sense of unsafety and uncertainty. Safety as a principle addresses the initial interaction with the environment: is it welcoming enough to make someone feel secure from the moment they enter? A sense of safety is critical, as Virginia Satir once said, "We need to feel safe before we can venture into the world's past." This emphasises how fundamental safety is in fostering an atmosphere where healing can begin.

A safe environment is one where individuals are shielded from further harm and can freely express their feelings and experiences without the risk of judgment or triggering past trauma. It involves both the physical setup—such as private, comfortable spaces that ensure confidentiality the individuals—and the emotional tone set by the staff, which should convey warmth and acceptance.

Moreover, safety within trauma-informed practice means consistently checking that the space remains secure and supportive. It requires attentiveness to changes in individual needs and adapting the environment accordingly. For example, asking feedback about the space's comfort or emotional impact can be instrumental in maintaining this safety.

In this secure setting, individuals can explore their vulnerabilities and begin the process of healing. As Judith Lewis Herman eloquently puts it, "The guarantee of safety in a therapeutic relationship not only protects, but also offers patients a microcosm of a better world." Thus, the principle of safety is not just about protection; it's about creating a foundation for transformative experiences and growth in a supportive environment.

Trust

Trust is vital in forging a strong, supportive relationship between service providers and those they help. It hinges on the service's ability to be sensitive and responsive to the specific needs of its users. Establishing trust involves more than just meeting expectations; it's about creating a bond that reassures individuals they are in a safe and reliable environment where their needs and voices are heard and respected.

Sensitivity in this context means understanding the emotional and practical needs of individuals, recognising their vulnerabilities without making them feel exposed or uncomfortable. Reliability relates to the consistency of care and support provided, where individuals can depend on the same high level of attention and responsiveness at each interaction. Transparency is crucial for trust as well; it involves clear communication about the processes, what one can expect, and the reasons behind certain decisions or methods. This openness helps demystify the process of care and reduces anxiety about the unknown.

Stephen Covey once stated, "Trust is the glue of life. It's the most essential ingredient in effective communication. It's the foundational principle that holds all relationships." In the context of trauma-informed practice, trust not only supports effective communication but also strengthens the therapeutic relationship. It encourages individuals to engage more openly and fully with the process, knowing that they are not only understood but also supported in a manner that respects their individual journey.

Building trust also requires an ongoing effort to adapt and respond to feedback, showing that the service does not just operate on a set protocol but is dynamically attuned to the evolving needs of those it serves. When individuals see and feel this level of commitment, trust deepens, enhancing their engagement and the overall effectiveness of the treatment or support they receive.

In summary, trust in trauma-informed practice is about creating a reliable, transparent, and sensitive environment that consistently meets the needs of its users. This principle is fundamental in ensuring that individuals feel secure and valued, facilitating a more effective and meaningful healing process.

Choice

The principle of choice is crucial in trauma-informed practice, as it empowers individuals by returning control over their healing journey. This facet of care is about ensuring that people have the freedom to choose from a variety of what repair and care means to and support mechanisms. By offering choices, services can help restore the autonomy that trauma may have compromised, reinforcing individuals' capacity to make decisions for themselves.

Choice is integral to the healing process because it addresses a common effect of trauma—the feeling of powerlessness. When individuals are able to make their own choices, they regain a sense of control over their lives, which is a critical step towards recovery. This empowerment through choice can significantly enhance the effectiveness of therapy or support, as individuals are more likely to engage with treatments and interventions they have actively selected.

Providing options also involves educating individuals about the different available pathways. This education should be delivered in a clear, understandable manner, enabling those seeking help to make informed decisions based on their needs, preferences, and goals. As Eleanor Roosevelt once said, "Freedom makes a huge requirement of every human being. With freedom comes responsibility." Thus, by offering choices, trauma-informed services not only grant freedom but also encourage responsibility, enabling individuals to take an active role in their recovery and future well-being.

Moreover, choice should be tailored to reflect individual circumstances, considering factors such as cultural backgrounds, personal values, and specific life experiences. This personalised approach ensures that the choices provided are relevant and meaningful, further enhancing the sense of control and empowerment for each person.

In sum, the principle of choice in trauma-informed practice is about more than just providing options; it's about respecting individuals' right to determine their own therapeutic path and supporting them in navigating these choices. This not only helps rebuild autonomy but also fosters a deeper engagement with the healing process, ultimately leading to more positive outcomes.

Collaboration

Collaboration is a central tenet of trauma-informed practice, emphasising the importance of working with individuals rather than for them. This approach fosters a partnership dynamic where the perspectives and input of those receiving support are not only welcomed but also regarded as crucial to the healing process. Such collaboration ensures that individuals are not passive recipients of care but active participants in their own recovery journey.

This collaborative approach is rooted in the belief that those experiencing trauma hold the key insights into their own needs and recovery. It recognises their inherent expertise on their personal experiences and challenges. By valuing this knowledge, service providers can work alongside individuals, co-creating a recovery plan that reflects their unique circumstances and aspirations. As Helen Keller aptly put it, "Alone we can do so little; together we can do so much." This sentiment underscores the power of collaborative efforts in achieving significant, sustainable recovery outcomes.

Engaging individuals in decision-making and planning not only empowers them but also enhances the relevance and effectiveness of the support provided. Collaboration involves continuous dialogue, where feedback is actively sought and used to adjust and refine the approach as needed. This dynamic process of communication and adjustment promotes a sense of shared effort and mutual goal-setting.

Moreover, effective collaboration requires transparency and openness from all parties involved. It builds trust and reinforces the therapeutic alliance, creating a stronger, more supportive relationship. Service providers must maintain a flexible and responsive attitude, adapting to the evolving needs and insights of those they assist.

In practice, collaboration might look like regular review sessions where feedback on the treatment's effectiveness and the individual's comfort with the process are openly discussed. It could also involve joint problem-solving sessions where challenges are addressed, and solutions are formulated together.

Ultimately, collaboration with community in trauma-informed practice is about embodying a partnership model that respects and harnesses the value of everyone's contributions. It ensures that reparative quest and recovery are not something imposed but is a shared journey towards healing, with each person's dignity and agency upheld throughout the process.

Empowerment

Empowerment stands as a cornerstone of trauma-informed practice, pivotal in helping individuals and communities regain control and authority over their own lives. This principle is essential because trauma often leaves individuals feeling powerless, communities overwhelmed by their experiences and circumstances. Empowerment in this context means enabling them to discover and utilize their inner strengths, thereby restoring their sense of self-efficacy and control.

This empowerment is achieved through strength-based approaches that focus on what individuals can do rather than what they cannot. By identifying and building upon existing resources and resilience, practitioners can help communities and individuals see themselves as capable and robust, which is vital for their recovery. As the famous saying by Alice Walker goes, "The most common way people give up their power is by thinking they don't have any." Therefore, the role of trauma-informed practice is to help individuals realise and harness the power they already possess.

Empowering communities and individuals involves more than just acknowledging their strengths; it includes actively involving them in their healing processes. This can be facilitated by setting goals that they are motivated to achieve, providing skills training that enhances their capabilities, or simply offering choices that allow them to navigate their recovery path. Each of these actions reinforces their autonomy and promotes a sense of accomplishment and independence.

Moreover, empowerment is also about fostering a supportive environment where individuals feel safe to express their thoughts and emotions without fear of judgment. This includes validating their feelings and experiences, which is crucial for healing. Validation confirms that their responses are understandable and justified, which can be incredibly affirming for those who has experienced trauma.

Furthermore, empowerment extends beyond individual interactions and encompasses the broader social context of an individual's life. This might involve advocating for changes in the social or institutional systems that impact them, helping them access community resources, or supporting them in building social networks. These broader actions ensure that empowerment is not just an internal feeling but a tangible reality reflected in all aspects of their life.

In summary, empowerment in trauma-informed practice is about encouraging and facilitating a process where communities and individuals can reclaim their lives through recognition and reinforcement of their strengths, autonomy, and capacity to effect change. It's about transforming the narrative from one of vulnerability to one of resilience and proactive engagement with life.

Respect for Diversity

Respect for diversity is a fundamental principle in trauma-informed practice, emphasizing the importance of acknowledging and valuing the diverse backgrounds and experiences that individuals bring to the table. This principle is crucial because each person's experience of trauma is influenced by their unique cultural, ethnic, gender, age, sexual orientation, and religious contexts. Recognizing this diversity not only enhances the therapeutic relationship but also ensures that the support provided is genuinely effective and sensitive to individual needs.

In practice, respecting diversity means services must be adaptive and flexible, intentionally designed to meet people where they are. This involves more than just an awareness of different cultural norms and values; it requires active efforts to integrate this understanding into all aspects of service delivery. As Audre Lorde famously said, "It is not our differences that divide us. It is our inability to recognize, accept, and celebrate those differences." In the context of trauma-informed care, this celebration of differences is operationalized through person-alised approaches that respect and utilize the strengths inherent in each person's background.

To respect diversity effectively, practitioners need to cultivate cultural competence, which involves an ongoing commitment to expanding one's understanding and sensitivity towards the cultural contexts of those they serve. This can include training on cultural awareness and humility, seeking knowledge about the communities represented by their clients, and actively challenging any biases or assumptions that might affect their practice.

Moreover, adapting and tailoring support can also mean providing language-appropriate services, considering traditional healing practices, and being mindful of historical traumas that may affect entire communities. For example, offering translation services or incorporating community-specific rituals into treatment can make a substantial difference in how individuals engage with and benefit from support.

Respect for diversity also entails creating an inclusive environment where all individuals feel seen, heard, and respected. This means ensuring that service settings are accessible to everyone, regardless of physical ability, and that materials and resources reflect the diverse populations served. It's about making everyone feel welcome and valued, reinforcing that their identity and experiences are not just recognized but are integral to their recovery journey.

Ultimately, respecting diversity within trauma-informed practice is about more than just compliance or surface-level inclusion; it's about embedding a deep respect for all individuals into the fabric of every interaction. By doing so, services not only become more effective but also act as powerful affirmations of each person's worth and dignity, significantly enriching the therapeutic process and outcomes.

Each of these principles, currently endorsed by many psychologists, psychiatrists and physicians, plays a vital role in creating an effective trauma-informed environment that fosters healing, resilience, and recovery.

Trauma and Violence-Informed Practice

While trauma-informed practice emphasizes creating safe environments and understanding the impact of trauma, trauma and violence-informed practice expands on these concepts. According to Varcoe et al. (2016), this approach accounts for the intersecting impacts of systemic and interpersonal violence and structural inequities on an individual's life. It adopts an intersectional perspective to recognise both current and historical experiences of violence. This ensures that problems are not viewed as originating within the individual but rather, in part, as adaptations and predictable outcomes of trauma and violence they have experienced.

Trauma-Informed Services

Trauma-informed services are specifically designed to accommodate the possibility that both service users and providers may have experienced trauma. These services acknowledge that trauma manifests uniquely across individuals, influencing them physically, emotionally, psychologically, behaviourally, socially, and interpersonally. While not necessarily treating trauma directly, trauma-informed services aim to ensure that their interactions do not trigger further trauma, harm, or distress.

This goal is achieved by embedding principles and values that promote well-being into every aspect of the service environment. This includes the workforce culture, policies, and practices, ensuring they are dynamic and reflective. Furthermore, trauma-informed services strive to create relationships and environments where individuals feel safe to disclose and discuss their trauma experiences.

As defined by SAMHSA (2014), a program, organisation, or system that is trauma-informed "realises the widespread impact of trauma and understands potential paths to recovery; recognises the signs and symptoms of trauma in clients, families, staff, and others involved with the system; and responds by fully integrating knowledge about trauma into policies, procedures, and practices, and seeks to actively resist re-traumatization."

Trauma-Specific Services

Trauma-specific services go a step further by providing therapeutic interventions specifically designed to support the healing and recovery of individuals based on their unique trauma experiences and needs. Although not all trauma-informed services are trauma-specific, it is essential that all trauma-specific services maintain a trauma-informed approach to be truly effective. This alignment ensures that the specific needs of individuals are met with appropriate, sensitive, and supportive care that aids in their recovery process.

This delineation between trauma-informed and trauma-specific services highlights a nuanced understanding of trauma care, ensuring that all practices, whether general or specific, maintain a core commitment to understanding and addressing the effects of trauma in a holistic and informed manner.

The exploration of trauma-informed and trauma and violence-informed practices reveals a progressive understanding of how deeply trauma and violence can affect individuals across various aspects of their lives. By adopting these approaches, we acknowledge that creating a supportive environment extends beyond merely avoiding triggers; it involves actively constructing a setting that empowers, respects, and facilitates healing for all involved including perpetrators of violence.

Trauma-informed practices, whether in general services or specific therapeutic interventions, provide a framework that expects and accommodates the presence of trauma in both community level and individuals level. These practices are designed to recognise and respond to the signs of trauma in a way that integrates knowledge into all facets of service delivery—from policy to practice—thereby fostering environments that resist re-traumatization and promote repair and recovery.

The significance of these practices is amplified in trauma and violence-informed approaches, which consider the additional layers of interpersonal and systemic violence and structural inequities. These practices incorporate an intersectional lens, ensuring that the solutions and supports provided are not only relevant and effective but also just and equitable.

Ultimately, the goal is to create spaces—whether in health-care, social services, or community support systems—that are not just safe but are also understanding, accommodating, and responsive to the complexities of trauma. By doing so, we can help communities and individuals navigate their healing journeys more effectively and with the dignity they deserve. This holistic and empathetic approach underlines the importance of viewing trauma recovery not just as a process of managing symptoms, but as a path to improve systems, servicers, regaining strength, agency, and empowerment.

CHAPTER 18

CONCLUSION

As we stand at the threshold of understanding, the concluding chapter of our exploration unfolds—a harmonious blend of reflection, revelation, and reclamation. This journey, marked by the echoes of violence and the resilience of the human spirit, beckons us to a higher calling—a path paved with empathy, unity, and unwavering solidarity.

Through the lens of South Sudanese experiences—echoed in the narratives of trauma, displacement, and the indomitable quest for peace—we have ventured deep into the heart of human suffering and redemption. Each chapter has unfurled layers of complexity, inviting us to confront our shared vulnerabilities and strengths.

The flow of the chapters artfully constructs a narrative that is both profound and transformative, guiding the reader through a journey that delves deep into the heart of violence, trauma, and ultimately, healing. Beginning with Chapter 1, "Unravelling the Threads of Violence and Trauma," the stage is set within the intimate confines of the home, extending into the vast expanse of societal violence, laying the groundwork for understanding the pervasive nature of trauma within South Sudanese communities.

As the narrative unfolds into Chapter 2, "A Road from Hell," we dive into the turbulent history of South Sudan, exposing the scars left by violence and setting the scene for a deeper exploration of its lasting effects. The journey then leads us to Chapter 3, "Colonial Inspired Civil Wars," where the historical roots of conflict are examined, revealing how colonial legacies have shaped the psyche and social fabric of the nation and its people.

Chapter 4, "War and Famine," presents a harrowing depiction of the devastating effects of conflict on human life, weaving together the physical and psychological traumas endured by communities caught in the crossfire. The narrative then transitions to Chapter 5, "Our Minds are Damaged," focusing on the mental and emotional scars borne from such violence, offering personal and collective accounts that bring the reader closer to the human experience of trauma.

In Chapter 6, "Community Violence Trauma," the book explores the phenomenon of community violence within oppressed communities, shedding light on how internalized trauma perpetuates cycles of violence. This exploration of internal dynamics leads into Chapter 7, "Migration and Trauma," which shifts the focus to the diaspora, discussing the challenges of resettlement and the struggle to heal while carrying the burdens of past wounds.

Chapter 8, "The Past In The Present," reflects on historical trauma, connecting past violence to contemporary experiences within South Sudanese communities, emphasizing the enduring impact of these traumas. The narrative deepens with Chapter 9, "Structural Violence Trauma," examining broader societal and systemic inequalities that perpetuate trauma, emphasizing the need for structural change. Chapter 10, "Classism & the Shame of Poverty," discussed the struggles that comes with being from a lower socioeconomic status and the shames classism brings into our society.

The book then delves into gender dynamics with Chapter 11, "Traumatised Masculinities Spawn Violence," discussing societal expectations around masculinity and their role in fuelling violence. Chapter 12, "Women Violence," further explores the unique pressures and challenges faced by women, highlighting the complexity of gender in the context of violence and healing.

In Chapter 13, "Filicide," a poignant case study serves as a focal point for discussing the extreme actions that can result from personal trauma and societal pressures. This leads into Chapter 14, "Evil or Illness," where the book contemplates the nature of violence, fostering a discussion around understanding, empathy, and healing.

Chapter 15, "Dead But Not Buried," addresses the psychological impact of war on veterans, portraying the living death experienced by those haunted by the horrors of conflict.

Chapter 16, "Repair," offers a vision for the future, advocating for comprehensive, trauma-informed approaches to healing that address the multifaceted nature of violence and its repercussions.

Through this progression of chapters, the book weaves a narrative that is at once heartbreaking and hopeful, offering insights into the complexities of violence and trauma while guiding the reader toward a deeper understanding and empathy. It culminates in a call to action, urging us towards healing, transformation, and ultimately, peace.

As our journey progressed, we delved into the profound challenges faced by refugees, exploring the delicate interplay of migration and trauma. Here, we encountered the resilience of the human spirit, striving for renewal amidst the remnants of war and loss.

In chapters exploring the dynamics of masculinity and the unique trials of women, we were invited to reflect on the gendered dimensions of violence and healing. The poignant stories of veterans—"Dead But Not Buried"—and the clarion call for "Repair" illuminated the path towards reconciliation and growth.

In confronting the complexities of violence, we have traversed a landscape marked by sorrow and hope, darkness and light. Our exploration has revealed the urgent need for a trauma-informed approach to violence—one that recognizes the intertwined narratives of individual and collective trauma and seeks to forge pathways to healing and peace.

The final note of this symphony calls us to action, urging

us to embrace our shared humanity and work collaboratively towards a future where compassion reigns supreme. It beckons us to become architects of empathy, crafting an orchestra of healing where every note resonates with the power of understanding and resilience.

As we close this chapter, let us hold fast to the vision of a world where the echoes of violence are transformed into melodies of peace and reconciliation. Together, we can compose a new symphony—one where the harmonies of healing and hope rise triumphant, guiding us towards a future illuminated by the light of compassion and unity.

In this work of healing, let us forge a legacy of love, understanding, and collective endeavour. As custodians of the future, we possess the power to mend the fabric of our communities, weaving together a tapestry where the wounds of the past forge the foundation for a harmonious and resilient tomorrow.

With hearts open and spirits lifted, we journey forth, guided by the beacon of empathy and the shared resolve to transcend the shadows of trauma. The symphony of humanity awaits its crescendo of harmony, and together, we are the composers of this new dawn—where violence fades into memory, and healing blossoms across the tapestry of our shared existence. Finally, chapter 17 offers some possible approaches for trauma-informed practice with main pillars that underscore a trauma-informed approach for and with people and communities with experiences of trauma to facilitate safer interventions and preventions.

ACKNOWLEDGEMENTS

To the South Sudanese communities, home and abroad, thank you for always welcoming me into your homes, lives, and experiences, past and present. Without you, my work would have no meaning and would have not been so close to my heart. Thank you for your vulnerabilities and trust in me whenever I call upon you. I am deeply grateful for how much you entrusted me with your stories.

To Peter Lual Deng from Africa World Books Publishing, your encouragement and support have aided the birth of this book. Your guidance has enabled me to achieve more than I thought possible in such a short amount of time.

To my colleagues, family and friends, thank you all very much for your support.

BIBLIOGRAPHY

Albino, O. (1970). The Sudan: A Southern Viewpoint. Oxford: Oxford University Press.

Allely, C. S. (2020). *The psychology of extreme violence a case study approach to serial homicide, mass shooting, school shooting and lone-actor terrorism.* London New York Routledge, Taylor & Francis Group.

Anser, M. K., & Yousaf, Z. (2020). Dynamic Linkages between poverty, inequality, crime, and Social Expenditures in a Panel of 16 countries: two-step GMM Estimates. *Journal of Economic Structures, 9*(1). https://doi.org/10.1186/s40008-020-00220-6

Anyieth, A. K. (2021). *South Sudanese Manhood and Family Crisis in the Diaspora.* Africa World Book Inc.

Anyieth, A. K. (2022). *Unknown.* Text Publishing.

Atkinson, J. (2002). *Trauma trails: Recreating song lines: The transgenerational effects of trauma in Indigenous Australia.* Spinifex Press.

Australian Human Rights Commission. (2011). Lateral violence in Aboriginal and Torres Strait Islander communities – *Social Justice Report* 2011.

Ben-Ezra, M., Goodwin, R., Leshem, E., & Hamama-Raz, Y. (2023). PTSD symptoms among civilians being displaced inside and outside the Ukraine during the 2022 Russian invasion. *Psychiatry Research*, *320*, 115011. https://doi.org/10.1016/j.psychres.2022.115011

Browning, C. R. (2017). *Ordinary men : reserve police battalion 101 and the final solution in Poland*. Harper Perennial.

Clare, A. W. (1969). 'Is aggression instinctive'? Studies 58, 158 – 165

Clark, K. B. (1989). *Dark ghetto : dilemmas of social power* (2nd ed., 1st Wesleyan ed). Wesleyan University Press.

De Courson, B., & Nettle, D. (2021). Why do inequality and deprivation produce high crime and low trust? *Scientific Reports*, *11*(1), 1–11. https://doi.org/10.1038/s41598-020-80897-8

Demuth, S., & Brown, S. L. (2004). Family Structure, Family Processes, and Adolescent Delinquency: The Significance of Parental Absence Versus Parental Gender. *Journal of Research in Crime and Delinquency*, *41*(1), 58-81. https://doi.org/10.1177/0022427803256236

Deng, F.M. (2020). 'Green is the colour of the Master, The Legacy of Slavery and the Crisis of National Identity in Modern Sudan'. https://glc.yale.edu/sites/default/files/files/events/cbss/Deng.pd

Dong. B. Egger, PH, Guo, Y .(2020). Is poverty the mother

of crime? Evidence from homicide rates in China. PLoS ONE 15(5): e0233034. https://doi.org/10.1371/journal. pone.0233034

Door Konrad Lorenz. (1966). *On aggression*. Harcourt, Brace & World.

Duncan, G. J., & Brooks-Gunn, J. (2000). Family Poverty, Welfare Reform, and Child Development. *Child Development*, *71*(1), 188–196. https://doi. org/10.1111/1467-8624.00133

Farrell, W., & Gray, J. (2019). *The boy crisis : why our boys are struggling and what we can do about it*. Dallas, Texas Benbella Books.

Fields R. D. (2019). THE ROOTS OF HUMAN AGGRESSION: Experiments in humans and animals have started to identify how violent behaviors begin in the brain. *Scientific American, 320*(5), 65–71.

Frankland, R. Bamblett, M. Lewis, P & Trotter, R. (2010). *This is "Forever Business": A Framework for Maintaining and Restoring Cultural Safety in Aboriginal Victoria*, Victorian Aboriginal Child Care Agency (2010), p 19.

Frantz Fanon. (1970). *Black skin, white masks*. Paladin.

Freud S. (1915). *Instincts and their vicissitudes. S. E.* 14: 117–140. London: Hogarth.

Gebremikael, F. (2003). The relationship of crime and poverty. *Journal of the Alabama Academy of Science, 74*(2), 104. https://link.gale.com/apps/docA115228138A-ONE?u=anon~cce9106d&sid=googleScholar&x-

id=c765e5d8

Gilligan, J. (2001). *Preventing violence.* Thames & Hudson.

Grier, W. H., & Cobbs, P. M. (1969). *Black Rage.* Bantam Books.

Heide Rieder, & Thomas Elbert. (2013). The relationship between organized violence, family violence and mental health: findings from a community-based survey in Muhanga, Southern Rwanda. *European Journal of Psychotraumatology, 4*(0), 1–10. https://doi.org/10.3402/ejpt.v4i0.21329

Herman, J. L. (2015). *Trauma and recovery: Aftermath of Violence from Domestic Abuse to Political Terror.* Basicbooks.

Hintjens, H. M. (1999). Explaining the 1994 genocide in Rwanda. *The Journal of Modern African Studies, 37*(2), 241–286. https://doi.org/10.1017/s0022278x99003018

Holt, P.M. (1956). 'Sudanese Nationalism and Self-Determination, Part II'. Middle East Journal, Vol. 10, No. 4, pp. 368–378.

Hynd, B., & de Waal, A. (1997). Famine Crimes: Politics and the Disaster Relief Industry in Africa. *Canadian Journal of African Studies, 31*(3), 586. https://doi.org/10.2307/486205

Johnson, D. (2003). The Root Causes of Sudan's Civil Wars. Indiana University Press.

Judith Lewis Herman. (1997). *Trauma and recovery : the aftermath of violence--from domestic abuse to political terror.* Basic Books.

Kelly, L. (1988). *Surviving sexual violence.* University Of Minnesota Press.

Khalid, M. (1990). The Government They Deserve: The Role of the Elite in Sudan's Political Evolution. London: Kegan Paul.

Khalid, M. (2003). War and Peace in Sudan: A Tale of Two Countries. London: Keegan Paul Ltd.

Luther, L. B. (1922). "Instincts and the Psychoanalysts." *Journal of Abnormal Psychology and Social Psychology*, XVII: 350-366.

Manning W. D., Lamb K. A. (2003). Adolescent well-being in cohabiting, married, and single-parent families. *Journal of Marriage and Family*, 65(4), 876-893.

Manning, W.D. and Brown, S. (2003). Children's Economic Well-Being in Married and Cohabiting Parent Families. *Journal of Marriage and Family*, 68. pp.345-362.

Mayo, D.N. (1994). 'The British Southern Policy in Sudan: An Inquiry into the Closed District Ordinances (1914–1946)'. Northeast African Studies, Vol. 1, No. 2-3, pp. 165–185.

McLanahan, S., & Sandefur, G. (1994). *Growing up with a single parent: What hurts, what helps.* Harvard University Press. https://doi.org/10.2307/585308

Miller, J. L., & Knudsen, D. D. (2007). *Family abuse and violence : a social problems perspective.* Altamira Press.

Miller, J. L., & Knudsen, D. D. (2007). *Family abuse and violence: a social problems perspective.* Altamira Press.

Murthy, R. S., & Lakshminarayana, R. (2006). Mental health consequences of war: a brief review of research findings. *World psychiatry : official journal of the World Psychiatric Association (WPA)*, 5(1), 25–30.

Rahim, A. M. (1966). 'The Development of British Policy in the Southern Sudan 1899–1947'. Middle Eastern Studies, Vol. 2, No. 3, pp. 227–249.

Rhodes, R. (2015). *Why They Kill*. Vintage.

Sampson, R. J., & Laub, J. H. (1994). Urban Poverty and the Family Context of Delinquency: A New Look at Structure and Process in a Classic Study. *Child Development*, 65(2), 523. https://doi.org/10.2307/1131400

Stritzel, H., Gonzalez, C. S., Cavanagh, S. E., & Crosnoe, R. (2021). Family Structure and Secondary Exposure to Violence in the Context of Varying Neighborhood Risks and Resources. *Socius : sociological research for a dynamic world*, 7, 10.1177/2378023121992941. https://doi.org/10.1177/2378023121992941

Tilly, C. (2003). The Politics of Collective Violence. New York: Cambridge University Press.

United Nations High Commissioner for Refugees. (2024). South Sudan Situation. South Sudan situation | Global Focus (unhcr.org)

Wilson, E. O. (1980). *Sociobiology*.

Yoder, J. R., Brisson, D., & Lopez, A. (2016). Moving Beyond Fatherhood Involvement: The Association Between Father-Child Relationship Quality and Youth Delinquency Trajectories. *Family Relations*, 65(3), 462–476. https://doi.org/10.1111/fare.12197

INDEX

www.ingramcontent.com/pod-product-compliance
Lightning Source LLC
Chambersburg PA
CBHW021856020426
42334CB00013B/357